Hatfield Polytechnic

Wall Hall Campus
Aldenham , Watford
Herts WD2 8AT

This book must be returned o
on or before the last d

WILLIAM COBBETT

COBBETT

Selections

With Hazlitt's Essay

and other critical estimates

With an Introduction and Notes by

A. M. D. HUGHES

OXFORD
AT THE CLARENDON PRESS

Oxford University Press, Amen House, London E.C.4

GLASGOW NEW YORK TORONTO MELBOURNE WELLINGTON
BOMBAY CALCUTTA MADRAS KARACHI KUALA LUMPUR
CAPE TOWN IBADAN NAIROBI ACCRA

FIRST EDITION 1923
REPRINTED 1925, 1935, 1940, 1946, 1951, 1961

PRINTED IN GREAT BRITAIN

CONTENTS

2179·17

INTRODUCTION

IT is a familiar piece of history that the industrial centres of England grew up in the main from small beginnings in a period not much longer than the Napoleonic wars, presenting suddenly all the tasks of a modern government to men unfit and unready for them ; and that these problems were solved only in a measure after a period of intense suffering. But few besides historical students are aware that, between the middle of the eighteenth century and that of the nineteenth, a revolution came about that put an end to the ancient order of village life with its social amenities and its physical well-being. It is reckoned that in the beginning of the eighteenth century 80 per cent. of English land was in private ownership, and chiefly in big estates ; but 20 per cent. was occupied on the mediaeval system of commonage. The common land was arable and meadow and waste. The arable was divided into strips, which were owned by individuals, singly or in lots of many or few, but cultivated uniformly and by agreement, and thrown open for pasturage after the harvest. The meadow was likewise distributed among the owners of the strips, and thrown open after the carrying of the hay ; and the waste was open, of course, at all times. The tenancy of a cottage frequently carried with it the right of pasture and forage on the waste, and perhaps also on the meadow, when released. The result was that rural society ranged gradually from the big landowner to the bigger and lesser yeomen (freeholders or tenants) and thence to the peasants, no gulf dividing landowner and labourer, for the same man

might be both; that the landless cottager was enabled by
the commonage to save money and buy a strip; that the
picture of social contentment in *The Deserted Village*, relating to the conditions of the first half of the century, was
not altogether a roseate fiction. The enclosures, by which
the aristocracy of the time incorporated the bulk of the
commons with their own estates, were comparatively infre-
quent till after 1760, but then they came apace; and when
Cobbett died in 1835, the separation of landowner, farmer,
and labourer was complete, and the labourer had lost his
little supplements and the privileges which had enabled
him to rise. Whatever may be said for the enclosures (and
much has been said), they were the ruin of the social
dispensation which is known as ' Merry England '.[1]

The revolution was aggravated by other things, which
loom bigger in this book. The wars enhanced the price of
food, and piled up taxes both for the needs of the hour and
for the interest on huge loans. They swelled the profits
of landlord and farmer, but not the workmen's wages;
and when the peace sent prices down, many of the men
who had grown accustomed to expensive living were quite
or nearly beggared, and the process set in in which a multi-
tude of the old masters of the land gave way to financial
speculators and industrial magnates, vanishing, as it
seemed, ' like caplins in the throats of the sharks '. To
Cobbett's mind, and not to his alone, these new masters,
living on the Funds, financing the industries, and pushing

[1] The reader may consult *The Village Labourer, 1760–1832*, by
J. L. Hammond and Barbara Hammond. The acts of enclosure
awarded lots of land to all commoners in proportion to their hold-
ings, including the cottagers with rights upon the waste; but the
expenses of the award and the duty of fencing the lots were too
much for the small people, whose acquisitions were soon snuffed
out, and were not in any case equivalent to the commonage. The
lord of the manor, who in legal fiction was the owner of the common,
was generally the biggest gainer by the deal.

forward the consolidation of the estates, were poisoning
the very element of a virile and happy people. It was
surely, as he thought, the business of the aristocracy first
to redress their own injustices, and then, by protective
laws, and even by repudiating the Debt, to stand between
the peasantry and the ' tax-eaters '. Instead of that, the
gentlemen of England seemed to him to have struck a tacit
bargain with the enemy, under which whoever had the
power might take or keep oppressive rights and gains.
The control of the House of Commons through the obsolete
franchise, the enormous system of pensions and sinecures,
the monopoly of local government, the practice by which
a very large number of the Anglican incumbents, many of
them with several benefices at once, lived on their tithes in
places like Bath and Cheltenham, and paid poor curates
to do their work : these were some of the old abuses for
the sake of which (as Cobbett thought) those who enjoyed
them had complied, to their own undoing, with the new.
This was THE THING—the undeclared confederacy of all
the rich and the well-provided to exhaust the poor. In
the rural districts, indeed, if the Funds were the root of the
evil, the squire's privileges were the thorns ; and more
especially the savage expedients to maintain the amenity
of their country seats—the heinous penalties on trespass,
the man-traps and spring-guns, the laws which, at a time
when poaching was the poor man's remedy for hunger,
doomed him for it to Botany Bay, or, for resisting his captors
in it, to a felon's death. Finally, in 1834, the ' wholesome
surgery ' of the Poor Law Amendment Act rescinded the
so-called Speenhamland System,[1] under which the wages
of farm labour were supplemented out of rates, and drove
great numbers of able-bodied men and women within the
workhouses, with the multiplication of which the whole
land was presently ringing.

[1] See note on p. 113.

Cobbett, seeing or so construing these things, burned against them with a wrath that weaned him from the delights of a country life, and bore him for thirty years through a splendid fight—through prison and exile and ' a hunt of obloquy '—for what he thought the strength of England,—that is, for the peasants, and thereby (whether they knew it or not) for the farmers and the lords of the land. Not indignation only drove his rasping pen into the eight and eighty volumes of the *Register*, but there flowed into it, like clear waters into a turbid stream, the joy and passion of an English yeoman, if ever one lived, for all that the new order seemed to menace or profane ; for the sights and sounds of homely countrysides, like his own Farnham and the Valley of the Wey, and for the robust humanities they had once sheltered when, in his own boyhood, he ploughed his father's fields, or ran many a day in blissful truancy after the hounds at the cost of a mere thrashing at bedtime. It is naturally on this element in his writing that the lover of ' pure literature ' will fasten, and it may be said that a wise selection would leave the politics and take the ' poetry '. Poetry it certainly is, if that means just the expression of keen feeling,—the musing pleasure of heart and eye in scenes like the high and dry downs enfolding in their warm hollows the villages and green meadows and tall trees ; in wild flowers and the songs of birds ; in ' the round red faces that you see in the wealds and the forests, where the labourer *will* have a meat pudding ' ; in solid houses, full rickyards, fat beasts ; for ' his eye desired grace and beauty and above both the green blade of corn '. The thoughts of many generations of men who lived and laboured in the sweet air of these places have broken into record in his books ; men of a sober blitheness, and a positive and noticing mind, casually overflowing with a deep lore in Nature's ways ; and it is goodly reading. But to miss out the underlying trouble of anger and grief would be robbing the melody of the counter-point, and taking what is noblest and most generous—what is even prophetic—from the writer's mind.

The critics here cited dwell on Cobbett's glaring faults. He was more than self-satisfied, truculent, overbearing ; and he often deserved what Coleridge said of him ;—' the rhinoceros of politics ', ' with the horn of brute strength on a nose of scorn and hate '. He changed his political attitudes often and abruptly ; and was in some things plainly wrong. He was wrong, for instance, it can hardly be disputed, on the Poor Law, and on the Debt. He propped his argument with notions of a mediaeval England swarming with population, in which the peasantry were abundantly fed, tended in sickness and trouble from the great monasteries,[1] and secured from hunger by a part of the tithes—tall constructions from matter picked up mostly in Fortescue and Lingard, and as confident as they were rash. All this and more can be charged on him. But the essay by Thorold Rogers, here included, is a corrective to the idea which Hazlitt and Lord Dalling have surely pressed too far—namely, that for pure pugnacity he could never keep to any view at all, but one day set up a theory, and knocked it down the next. Heine, who saw him in 1827 behaving fractiously at a public dinner, ' with his scolding red face and his radical laugh, venomous hate mingled with a mocking triumph ', has judged him in the same way. ' He is a chained house-dog, who falls with equal fury on everyone he does not know, often biting the best friends of the house, barking incessantly, and because of the incessantness not getting listened to, even when he barks at a real thief. Poor Cobbett, England's watch-dog !' But the truth partly is that he was slow to get his bearings in the political world, and the needle lunged and swayed before it came to rest. There was always, however, a consistent base to

[1] This is the point in his *History of the Protestant Reformation.*

his opinions, a body of invariable instincts and beliefs, which included, as Thorold Rogers tells us, keen insight into the economic malady. Indeed, we do not now need to be historians or economists to see plainly that in the main he was not only magnificent but right, and his ruling passion as reasonable as it was strong and pure. Under its generous heat, we forget the misjudgement or the misbehaviour, and think of him, with Coleridge,[1] as one of England's great educators, who, with his perfect mastery of the popular style, ' gave publicity to weighty truths ' by making them sun-clear and dinning them into all men's ears.

There is another and a surprising side to Cobbett. He tells us [2] how in his early teens, after hearing of the glory of Kew Gardens, he started secretly from Farnham one morning and tramped to Kew, in the hope of taking service in the grounds ; and at Richmond spent his last threepence, and resigned his supper, for a copy of *A Tale of a Tub*. The book was eagerly read and dearly treasured, till he lost it ' in a box that fell overboard in the Bay of Fundy ', with ' more pain than I have ever felt at losing thousands of pounds '. There was much to please him in Swift,—clearness, trenchancy, an imperious will, a grim cynicism, and with it

> the tenor of his mind
> To merit well of human kind.

But the free and open writing of the *Rural Rides* is very different from Swift's bare intensity and self-repression and self-disguise ; and the ideal of human living thrown out in *Gulliver* in despair and scorn is equally distant from the wholesome world of Cobbett's longing, a world that men had once created and might retrieve. There is, however,

---

[1] See his letter to T. Allsop, December 13, 1819.

[2] In a passage given at length in Mr. E. I. Carlyle's *William Cobbett* (p. 6).

a certain wistfulness in the longing, and rather more of looking back than looking forward. And his intermittent sense of beauty puts him now and then and for brief moments at the point of prophetic vision, in which, as in many other ways, he dimly anticipates the revolt under Ruskin and Morris from the whole fashion of our times. He believed like them that souls and minds, as well as bodies, thrive only in contact with Nature and in the open air, and wither under many books; that England was richest before the towns and factories came, ' when her faces were ruddy and her fields were green '; that better morality and more genius were produced in the quiet fixity of the mediaeval order, when a man grew old in one duty and sphere, in one spot and one house; that, binding men close together, not, as now, casting them loose, this order sweetened their relations with more kindness; that the great churches and other relics of the art which was then a common faculty and a perpetual solace bear witness to an abundance of power and joy; and that the way back to all these better things begins in political justice. Here was the fret of a disgust and a yearning which are strong in modern men, and an appeal deeper than argument. The reader may assent to Cobbett's policy more or less; but on the mean and false or the true and fair in men's arts and lives he speaks as one who *sees*. A finer wisdom plays like a casual flame over his plain Puritanism and stolid practicality; ' singular humanities ', in Carlyle's words, ' shine through his thick skin '; and sweetness comes forth out of the strong. For ' a vigorous . . . human-heartedness ', as Wordsworth once wrote, ' is the constituent principle of a true taste '.

COBBETT'S LIFE

1762 or 1763. William Cobbett, born at Farnham, son of George Cobbett, a farmer and inn-keeper. Is taught the three R's at an early age in a dame's school and by his father at home.

1774 (?). Travels on foot to London, without leave of his parents, and takes service in the Gardens at Kew. On the way buys with his last 3*d*. a copy of Swift's *Tale of a Tub*, which he repeatedly reads, and to which he feels himself indebted for ' a birth of intellect '.

1782. Visit to Portsmouth (pp. 36 f.).

1783 (May). Absconds to London, and works for some nine months as a lawyer's clerk.

1784. Enlists at Chatham in the 54th Foot. Learns grammar, reads assiduously, and becomes clerk to the commandant of the garrison.

1785–91. With his regiment in Nova Scotia and New Brunswick. In two years becomes sergeant-major.

1791 (December). Obtains his discharge on his return to England.

1792. Marries Ann Reid at Woolwich (February 5). Accuses officers of the 54th of peculation, supporting his charge by evidence secretly copied from the regimental accounts. Supposing the authorities to be in connivance with the accused, and himself in danger of false charges in a hostile court, takes refuge in France, and proceeds thence (October) to Philadelphia.

October 1792—June 1800. First residence in America. Lives at first by teaching English to French refugees in Philadelphia ; writes and publishes (1795) his *Tuteur Anglais*, or English grammar for French students, which has much vogue in France. Becomes (from June 1794) a pamphleteer on the side of the Federalists or Anglophil party, against the Francophil Democrats, and cordially denounces the French Revolution. In March 1795 assumes pseudonym of Peter Porcupine. Issues *The Political Censor*, a report of proceedings in Congress, with commentary (January 1796—January 1797). Opens a bookseller's shop in Philadelphia (July 1796), reveals his identity with Porcupine, and defies continual threats of violence from political opponents. Writes *Life and Adventures of Peter Porcupine* (August

1796) in self-defence. Defends Washington against attacks of Thomas Paine. Publishes *Porcupine's Gazette and Daily Advertiser* to support the Federals, denounce the French, and advocate an English Alliance (March 1797—January 1800). Heavily fined for libel on Benjamin Rush, a doctor whom he accused of quackery (December 1799). Leaves America in dudgeon.

1800. Arriving in London (July), is warmly welcomed by the Tories and the Ministry. Refuses the editorship of a government paper, and starts *The Porcupine* as an independent supporter of the Ministry in the war with France.

1801. Passionately opposes negotiations which ended in the Peace of Amiens. Refuses to join in the illumination of London on the prospect of peace, and has his windows broken and his office wrecked by the rabble. Exposes the weaknesses of the proposed Peace in the *Letters to Lord Hawkesbury*. In November disposes of *The Porcupine*, which did not pay its way. Publishes his American writings under the title *Porcupine's Works*.

1802. Launches the weekly *Political Register* (January), which continues to appear until June 1835. His house again assailed by the mob on signature of the Peace (March). The war renewed (May). Sentenced to a fine for attacking Addington's Ministry for conduct of Irish affairs. Begins publishing *Cobbett's Parliamentary Debates* (June).

1804 (April). Fall of the Addington Ministry. Fox, now in favour of the war, is excluded from office by the King's resentment, and joins the extreme Tories under Windham in opposition to the new Ministry of Pitt. Cobbett sides with the Opposition. He begins his war on the system of pensions and sinecures.

1805. Buys the farm called Fairthorn in the parish of Botley.

1806. Death of Pitt (January 23) and formation of the Ministry of All the Talents. Cobbett approves of the continuance of the war ; but, his mind being now centred on finance and internal reform, demands a domestic policy so radical that no Ministry of that date could have satisfied him. He goes over to the Radical party definitely and for good, and henceforth addresses not the men in power but the people at large. Stands for Honiton as an anti-bribery candidate at a by-election, but retires in favour of Lord Cochrane. Begins publishing *Cobbett's Parliamentary History of England* (completed April 1820).

1807 (March). The Tories come into power, led by Canning and

Castlereagh. Cobbett begins to urge the necessity of parliamentary reform and to assail the scandals of the electoral system. About the same time he modifies his attitude towards France and the war. Continual and damaging criticism of the conduct of government.

1809. Begins publishing *Cobbett's State Trials* (concluded 1826). Article in the *Register* (July 1) on the flogging of mutinous militiamen at Ely under a guard of Hanoverian soldiers.

1810. July 9, sentenced in King's Bench by Lord Ellenborough to a fine of £1,000 and two years' imprisonment for this article, and confined in Newgate, whence he continues the *Register*. Writes his letters entitled *Paper against Gold*, condemning paper money, but insisting that before the resumption of cash payments the National Debt must be abolished, lest the nation should pay in gold a debt standing in depreciated paper.

1812. Released (July). Begins to attack the system of tithes.

1816. The agricultural and industrial distress following the war revives the popularity of the *Register*, which had declined under the spell of the great victories. Cobbett commences itinerant speaker for parliamentary reform. His *Letter to the Luddites*, to dissuade labouring men from violence (November). The price of the *Register* reduced from 1s. 0½d. to 2d.; its circulation and authority much increased.

1817. Cobbett is advertised by a journal started by his enemies and entitled *Anti-Cobbett*. Suspension of the Habeas Corpus Act. Under stress of financial embarrassment and in fear of the Government, now armed with extraordinary powers, he absconds to America, and lands in New York in May.

May 1817 to November 1819. Second residence in America. Takes a farm at North Hempstead in Long Island. Publishes *A Year's Residence in the United States of America* (1818–19), and continues to direct the *Political Register*. Publishes *A Grammar of the English Language* (1818). Digs up the coffin of Thomas Paine, buried as a deist in waste land at New Rochelle, and takes the bones with him on returning to England, in order to bury them there, and so atone for his scurrilous *Life of Thomas Paine*, written (1796) in his Tory days. Cobbett and the bones greeted in England with derision. (The bones remained in his possession until his death, and were afterwards lost.)

1820. Cobbett severely injured by stamp duty imposed on periodicals by one of the Six Acts. Stands for Parliament at Coventry, and is defeated (March). Becomes bankrupt, sells the estate at Botley (June), and moves to Kensington. Passionately advocates the cause of Queen Caroline.

1820 to 1830. Period of greatest literary activity. *Cobbett's Monthly Sermons* (March 1821—March 1822), *Cottage Economy* (1821–22). His *Rural Rides* begin October 1821 ; continued occasionally to October 1832. *History of the Protestant Reformation in England and Ireland* (1824–5), *Woodlands* (1825), *The English Gardener* (1828), *Advice to Young Men* (1829–30). *Rural Rides*, reprinted from the *Register* (1830 ; second and extended edition issued by John Paul Cobbett, 1853).

1826 (July). Stands for Parliament at Preston and is defeated.

1830. Issues cheap monthly reprints of portions of the *Register* under the title *Cobbett's Twopenny Trash*. Widespread arson and disorder in the country districts.

1831 (July). Indicted in the Court of King's Bench on a charge of encouraging the rural disorders by an article in the *Register*, and conducts his own defence. The prosecution fails. (The last attempt by Government to coerce the press by legal action.) Cobbett takes Normanby Farm in Ash, Surrey.

1832. In general election following the Reform Bill returned to Parliament as independent member for Oldham, and, speaking frequently in the House ' with a dry, caustic, and rather drawling delivery . . . became rather a favourite with an audience which is only unforgiving when bored ' (Lord Dalling), but otherwise ineffective.

1834. Visits the south and west of Ireland, and is enthusiastically received. Publishes his *Legacy to Labourers* (December). Strongly opposes Poor Law Amendment Act.

1835. Elected to new Parliament for Oldham unopposed (January). Writes *A Legacy to Peel*, anticipating Peel's later reforms, and *A Legacy to Parsons* in favour of disestablishment. Dies on June 18 at Normanby Farm, and is buried in the churchyard at Farnham.

HAZLITT'S Essay

(First published in *Table Talk*, vol. i, 1821 ; afterwards in *The Spirit of the Age*, Second Edition, 1825.)

PEOPLE have about as substantial an idea of Cobbett as they have of Cribb. His blows are as hard, and he himself is as impenetrable. One has no notion of him as making use of a fine pen, but a great mutton-fist ; his style stuns his readers, and he ' fillips the ear of the public with a three-man beetle.' He is too much for any single newspaper antagonist, ' lays waste ' a city orator or Member of Parliament, and bears hard upon the Government itself. He is a kind of *fourth estate* in the politics of the country.   10

He is not only unquestionably the most powerful political writer of the present day, but one of the best writers in the language. He speaks and thinks plain, broad, downright English. He might be said to have the clearness of Swift, the naturalness of Defoe, and the picturesque satirical description of Mandeville : if all such comparisons were not impertinent. A really great and original writer is like nobody but himself. In one sense, Sterne was not a wit, nor Shakespeare a poet. It is easy to describe second-rate talents, because they fall into a class and enlist under 20 a standard : but first-rate powers defy calculation or comparison, and can be defined only by themselves. They are *sui generis*, and make the class to which they belong. I have tried half-a-dozen times to describe Burke's style without ever succeeding : its severe extravagance, its literal boldness, its matter-of-fact hyperboles, its running away with a subject and from it at the same time ; but there is no making it out, for there is no example of the

same thing any where else. We have no common measure
to refer to ; and his qualities contradict even themselves.

Cobbett is not so difficult. He has been compared to
Paine ; and so far it is true there are no two writers who
come more into juxtaposition from the nature of their
subjects, from the internal resources on which they draw,
and from the popular effect of their writings and their
adaptation (though that is a bad word in the present case)
to the capacity of every reader. But still, if we turn to
10 a volume of Paine's (his Common Sense or Rights of Man)
we are struck (not to say somewhat refreshed) by the
difference. Paine is a much more sententious writer than
Cobbett. You cannot open a page in any of his best and
earlier works without meeting with some maxim, some
antithetical and memorable saying, which is a sort of
starting-place for the argument, and the goal to which
it returns.

There is not a single *bon-mot*, a single sentence in Cobbett
that has ever been quoted again. If any thing is ever
20 quoted from him, it is an epithet of abuse or a nickname.
He is an excellent hand at invention in that way, and has
' damnable iteration in him.' What could be better than
his pestering Erskine year after year with his second title
of Baron Clackmannan ? He is rather too fond of such
phrases as *the Sons and Daughters of Corruption*. Paine
affected to reduce things to first principles, to announce
self-evident truths. Cobbett troubles himself about little
but the details and local circumstances. The first appeared
to have made up his mind beforehand to certain opinions,
30 and to try to find the most compendious and pointed
expressions for them : his successor appears to have no
clue, no fixed or leading principles, nor ever to have
thought on a question till he sits down to write about it.
But then there seems no end of his matters of fact and
raw materials, which are brought out in all their strength

and sharpness from not having been squared or frittered down or vamped up to suit a theory. He goes on with his descriptions and illustrations as if he would never come to a stop ; they have all the force of novelty with all the familiarity of old acquaintance. His knowledge grows out of the subject ; and his style is that of a man who has an absolute intuition of what he is talking about, and never thinks of any thing else. He deals in premises and speaks to evidence : the coming to a conclusion and summing up (which was Paine's forte) lies in a smaller compass. The one could not compose an elementary treatise on politics to become a manual for the popular reader ; nor could the other in all probability have kept up a weekly journal for the same number of years with the same spirit, interest and untired perseverance. Paine's writings are a sort of introduction to political arithmetic on a new plan ; Cobbett keeps a day-book, and makes an entry at full of all the occurrences and troublesome questions that start up throughout the year.

Cobbett with vast industry, vast information and the utmost power of making what he says intelligible, never seems to get at the beginning or come to the end of any question : Paine in a few short sentences seems by his peremptory manner ' to clear it from all controversy, past, present, and to come.' Paine takes a bird's-eye view of things ; Cobbett sticks close to them, inspects the component parts, and keeps fast hold of the smallest advantages they afford him. Or, if I might here be indulged in a pastoral allusion, Paine tries to enclose his ideas in a fold for security and repose ; Cobbett lets *his* pour out upon the plain like a flock of sheep to feed and batten. Cobbett is a pleasanter writer for those to read who do not agree with him ; for he is less dogmatical, goes more into the common grounds of fact and argument to which all appeal, is more desultory and various, and appears less to be driving at a previous conclusion than urged on by the force of present conviction. He is therefore tolerated by all parties, though he has made himself by turns obnoxious to all ; and even those he abuses read him. The Reformers read him when he was a Tory, and the Tories read him now that he is a Reformer. He must, I think, however, be *caviare* to the Whigs.

If he is less metaphysical and poetical than his celebrated prototype, he is more picturesque and dramatic. His episodes, which are numerous as they are pertinent, are striking, interesting, full of life and *naïveté*, minute, double measure running over, but never tedious—*nunquam suffla-minandus erat.* He is one of those writers who can never tire us, not even of himself ; and the reason is, he is always 'full of matter.' He never runs to lees, never gives us the vapid leavings of himself, is never 'weary, stale, and unprofitable,' but always setting out afresh on his journey, clearing away some old nuisance, and turning up new mould. His egotism is delightful, for there is no affectation in it. He does not talk of himself for lack of something to write about, but because some circumstance that has happened to himself is the best possible illustration of the subject ; and he is not the man to shrink from giving the best possible illustration of the subject from a squeamish delicacy. He likes both himself and his subject too well. He does not put himself before it, and say 'admire me first,' but places us in the same situation with himself, and makes us see all that he does. There is no blind-man's buff, no conscious hints, no awkward ventriloquism, no testimonies of applause, no abstract, senseless self-com-placency, no smuggled admiration of his own person by proxy. It is all plain and above-board.

He writes himself plain William Cobbett, strips himself quite as naked as any body could wish : in a word, his egotism is full of individuality, and has room for very

little vanity in it. We feel delighted, rub our hands, and
draw our chair to the fire, when we come to a passage of
this sort : we know it will be something new and good,
manly and simple, not the same insipid story of self over
again. We sit down at table with the writer, but it is of
a course of rich viands—flesh, fish, and wild fowl—and not
to a nominal entertainment, like that given by the Barmecide in the Arabian Nights, who put off his visitor with
calling for a number of exquisite things that never appeared
and with the honour of his company. Mr. Cobbett is not 10
a *make-believe* writer. His worst enemy cannot say that
of him. Still less is he a vulgar one. He must be a puny
commonplace critic indeed, who thinks him so. How fine
were the graphical descriptions he sent us from America :
what a transatlantic flavour, what a native *gusto*, what
a fine *sauce piquante* of contempt they were seasoned with !
If he had sat down to look at himself in the glass, instead
of looking about him like Adam in Paradise, he would not
have got up these articles in so capital a style. What
a noble account of his first breakfast after his arrival in 20
America ! It might serve for a month. There is no scene
on the stage more amusing.

How well he paints the gold and scarlet plumage of the
American birds, only to lament more pathetically the want
of the wild wood-notes of his native land ! The groves of
the Ohio that had just fallen beneath the axe's stroke,
'live in his description,' and the turnips that he trans-
planted from Botley 'look green ' in prose ! How well at
another time he describes the poor sheep that had got the
tick, and had tumbled down in the agonies of death ! It 30
is a portrait in the manner of Bewick, with the strength,
the simplicity, and feeling of that great naturalist. What
havoc he makes, when he pleases, of the curls of Dr. Parr's
wig and of the Whig consistency of Mr. —— ! His Grammar, too, is as entertaining as a story-book. He is too

hard, however, upon the style of others, and not enough
(sometimes) on his own.

As a political partisan, no one can stand against him.
With his brandished club, like Giant Despair in the
Pilgrim's Progress, he knocks out their brains : and not
only no individual, but no corrupt system, could hold out
against his powerful and repeated attacks. But with the
same weapon swung round like a flail, with which he levels
his antagonists, he lays his friends low, and puts his own
party *hors de combat.* This is a bad propensity and a worse
principle in political tactics, though a common one. If his
blows were straightforward and steadily directed to the
same object, no unpopular minister could live before him ;
instead of which he lays about right and left impartially
and remorselessly, makes a clear stage, has all the ring
to himself, and then runs out of it, just when he should
stand his ground. He throws his head into his adversary's
stomach, and takes away from him all inclination for the
fight, hits fair or foul, strikes at every thing, and as you
come up to his aid or stand ready to pursue his advantage,
trips up your heels or lays you sprawling, and pummels
you when down as much to his heart's content as ever the
Yanguesian carriers belaboured Rosinante with their pack-
staves. *' He has the back-trick simply the best of any man
in Illyria.'*

He pays off both scores of old friendship and new-
acquired enmity in a breath, in one perpetual volley, one
raking fire of ' arrowy sleet ' shot from his pen. However
his own reputation or the cause may suffer in consequence,
he cares not one pin about that, so that he disables all
who oppose or who pretend to help him. In fact, he
cannot bear success of any kind, not even of his own
views or party ; and if any principle were likely to become
popular, would turn round against it, to show his power
in shouldering it on one side. In short, wherever power is,

there is he against it : he naturally butts at all obstacles, as unicorns are attracted to oak-trees, and feels his own strength only by resistance to the opinions and wishes of the rest of the world. To sail with the stream, to agree with the company, is not his humour. If he could bring about a Reform in Parliament, the odds are that he would instantly fall foul of and try to mar his own handy-work ; and he quarrels with his own creatures as soon as he has written them into a little vogue—and a prison. I do not think this is vanity or fickleness so much as a pugnacious 10 disposition, that must have an antagonist power to contend with, and only finds itself at ease in systematic opposition. If it were not for this, the high towers and rotten places of the world would fall before the battering-ram of his hard-headed reasoning : but if he once found them totter-ing, he would apply his strength to prop them up, and disappoint the expectations of his followers. He cannot agree to any thing established, nor to set up any thing else in its stead. While it is established, he presses hard against it, because it presses upon him, at least in imagination. 20 Let it crumble under his grasp, and the motive to resistance is gone. He then requires some other grievance to set his face against.

His principle is repulsion, his nature contradiction : he is made up of mere antipathies ; an Ishmaelite indeed without a fellow. He is always playing at *hunt-the-slipper* in politics. He turns round upon whoever is next to him. The way to wean him from any opinion, and make him conceive an intolerable hatred against it, would be to place somebody near him who was perpetually dinning it in his 30 ears. When he is in England, he does nothing but abuse the Boroughmongers, and laugh at the whole system : when he is in America, he grows impatient of freedom and a republic. If he had stayed there a little longer, he would have become a loyal and a loving subject of his Majesty

King George IV. He lampooned the French Revolution
when it was hailed as the dawn of liberty by millions ; by
the time it was brought into almost universal ill-odour by
some means or other (partly no doubt by himself) he had
turned, with one or two or three others, staunch Bona-
partist. He is always of the militant, not of the triumphant
party : so far he bears a gallant show of magnanimity.
But his gallantry is hardly of the right stamp : it wants
principle. For though he is not servile or mercenary, he
10 is the victim of self-will. He must pull down and pull in
pieces : it is not in his disposition to do otherwise. It is
a pity ; for with his great talents he might do great things,
if he would go right forward to any useful object, make
thorough-stitch work of any question, or join hand and
heart with any principle. He changes his opinions as he
does his friends, and much on the same account. He has
no comfort in fixed principles : as soon as any thing is
settled in his own mind, he quarrels with it. He has no
satisfaction but in the chase after truth, runs a question
20 down, worries and kills it, then quits it like vermin, and
starts some new game, to lead him a new dance, and give
him a fresh breathing through bog and brake, with the
rabble yelping at his heels and the leaders perpetually at
fault.

This he calls sport-royal. He thinks it as good as cudgel-
playing or single-stick, or any thing else that has life in it.
He likes the cut and thrust, the falls, bruises and dry blows
of an argument : as to any good or useful results that may
come of the amicable settling of it, any one is welcome to
30 them for him. The amusement is over, when the matter
is once fairly decided.

There is another point of view in which this may be put.
I might say that Mr. Cobbett is a very honest man with
a total want of principle ; and I might explain this paradox
thus. I mean that he is, I think, in downright earnest in

what he says, in the part he takes at the time ; but, in
taking that part, he is led entirely by headstrong obstinacy,
caprice, novelty, pique or personal motive of some sort, and
not by a steadfast regard for truth or habitual anxiety for
what is right uppermost in his mind. He is not a feeble,
time-serving, shuffling advocate (no man could write as he
does who did not believe himself sincere), but his understanding is the dupe and slave of his momentary, violent
and irritable humours. He does not adopt an opinion
' deliberately or for money ' ; yet his conscience is at the 10
mercy of the first provocation he receives, of the first whim
he takes in his head. He sees things through the medium
of heat and passion, not with reference to any general
principles ; and his whole system of thinking is deranged
by the first object that strikes his fancy or sours his
temper.

One cause of this phenomenon is perhaps his want of
a regular education. He is a self-taught man, and has the
faults as well as excellences of that class of persons in their
most striking and glaring excess. It must be acknowledged 20
that the Editor of the Political Register (the *two-penny
trash*, as it was called, till a Bill passed the House to raise
the price to sixpence) is not ' the gentleman and scholar,'
though he has qualities that, with a little better management, would be worth (to the public) both those titles.
For want of knowing what has been discovered before him,
he has not certain general landmarks to refer to or a general
standard of thought to apply to individual cases. He relies
on his own acuteness and the immediate evidence, without
being acquainted with the comparative anatomy or philo- 30
sophical structure of opinion. He does not view things on
a large scale or at the horizon (dim and airy enough perhaps) ; but as they affect himself—close, palpable, tangible.
Whatever he finds out is his own, and he only knows what
he finds out. He is in the constant hurry and fever of

gestation : his brain teems incessantly with some fresh project. Every new light is the birth of a new system, the dawn of a new world to him. He is continually out-stripping and overreaching himself. The last opinion is the only true one. He is wiser to-day than he was yesterday. Why should he not be wiser to-morrow than he was to-day ?

Men of a learned education are not so sharp-witted as clever men without it ; but they know the balance of the human intellect better. If they are more stupid, they are 10 more steady, and are less liable to be led astray by their own sagacity and the overweening petulance of hard-earned and late-acquired wisdom. They do not fall in love with every meretricious extravagance at first sight, or mistake an old battered hypothesis for a vestal, because they are new to the ways of this old world. They do not seize upon it as a prize, but are safe from gross imposition by being as wise and no wiser than those who went before them.

Paine said on some occasion, ' What I have written, I have written,' as rendering any farther declaration of 20 his principles unnecessary. Not so Mr. Cobbett. What he has written is no rule to him what he is to write. He learns something every day, and every week he takes the field to maintain the opinions of the last six days against friend or foe. I doubt whether this outrageous inconsistency, this headstrong fickleness, this understood want of all rule and method, does not enable him to go on with the spirit, vigour and variety that he does. He is not pledged to repeat himself. Every new Register is a kind of new Prospectus. He blesses himself from all ties and shackles 30 on his understanding ; he has no mortgages on his brain ; his notions are free and unincumbered. If he was put in trammels, he might become a vile hack like so many more. But he gives himself ' ample scope and verge enough.' He takes both sides of a question, and maintains one as sturdily as the other. If nobody else can argue against

him, he is a very good match for himself. He writes better
in favour of reform than any body else; he used to write
better against it. Wherever he is, there is the tug of war,
the weight of the argument, the strength of abuse.

He is not like a man in danger of being *bed-rid* in his
faculties: he tosses and tumbles about his unwieldy bulk,
and when he is tired of lying on one side, relieves himself
by turning on the other. His shifting his point of view
from time to time not merely adds variety and greater
compass to his topics (so that the Political Register is an 10
armoury and magazine for all the materials and weapons
of political warfare): but it gives a greater zest and liveli-
ness to his manner of treating them. Mr. Cobbett takes
nothing for granted, as what he has proved before; he
does not write a book of reference. We see his ideas in
their first concoction, fermenting and overflowing with the
ebullitions of a lively conception. We look on at the
actual process, and are put in immediate possession of the
grounds and materials on which he forms his sanguine,
unsettled conclusions. He does not give us samples of 20
reasoning, but the whole solid mass, refuse and all.

> ' ——He pours out all as plain
> As downright Shippen or as old Montaigne.'

This is one cause of the clearness and force of his writings.
An argument does not stop to stagnate and muddle in his
brain, but passes at once to his paper. His ideas are served
up, like pancakes, hot and hot.

Fresh theories give him fresh courage. He is like a young
and lusty bridegroom, that divorces a favourite speculation
every morning, and marries a new one every night. He is 30
not wedded to his notions, not he. He has not one Mrs. Cobbett among all his opinions. He makes the most of the last
thought that has come in his way, seizes fast hold of it,
rumples it about in all directions with rough strong hands,

has his wicked will of it, takes a surfeit, and throws it
away. Our author's changing his opinions for new ones
is not so wonderful ; what is more remarkable is his felicity
in forgetting his old ones. He does not pretend to consistency (like Mr. Coleridge) ; he frankly disavows all
connection with himself. He feels no personal responsibility
in this way, and cuts a friend or principle with the same
decided indifference that Antipholis of Ephesus cuts Ægeon
of Syracuse. It is a hollow thing. The only time he ever
10 grew romantic was in bringing over the relics of Mr. Thomas
Paine with him from America, to go a progress with them
through the disaffected districts. Scarce had he landed in
Liverpool, when he left the bones of a great man to shift
for themselves ; and no sooner did he arrive in London,
than he made a speech to disclaim all participation in the
political and theological sentiments of his late idol, and to
place the whole stock of his admiration and enthusiasm
towards him to the account of his financial speculations,
and of his having predicted the fate of paper-money.
20   If he had erected a little gold statue to him, it might
have proved the sincerity of this assertion ; but to make
a martyr and a patron-saint of a man, and to dig up ' his
canonized bones ' in order to expose them as objects of
devotion to the rabble's gaze, asks something that has more
life and spirit in it, more mind and vivifying soul, than has
to do with any calculation of pounds, shillings, and pence !
The fact is, he *ratted* from his own project. He found the
thing not so ripe as he had expected. His heart failed
him ; his enthusiasm fled ; and he made his retraction.
30 His admiration is short-lived : his contempt only is rooted,
and his resentment lasting. The above was only one
instance of his building too much on practical *data*. He
has an ill habit of prophesying, and goes on, though still
deceived. The art of prophesying does not suit Mr. Cobbett's style. He has a knack of fixing names and times

and places. According to him, the Reformed Parliament
was to meet in March, 1818 ; it did not, and we heard no
more of the matter. When his predictions fail, he takes
no farther notice of them, but applies himself to new ones,
like the country-people, who turn to see what weather
there is in the almanac for the next week, though it has
been out in its reckoning every day of the last.

Mr. Cobbett is great in attack, not in defence : he cannot fight an up-hill battle. He will not bear the least
punishing. If any one turns upon him (which few people 10
like to do), he immediately turns tail. Like an overgrown
school-boy, he is so used to have it all his own way, that
he cannot submit to any thing like competition or a struggle
for the mastery : he must lay on all the blows, and take
none. He is bullying and cowardly ; a Big Ben in politics,
who will fall upon others and crush them by his weight,
but is not prepared for resistance, and is soon staggered
by a few smart blows. Whenever he has been set upon,
he has slunk out of the controversy. The Edinburgh
Review made (what is called) a dead set at him some years 20
ago, to which he only retorted by an eulogy on the superior
neatness of an English kitchen-garden to a Scotch one.
I remember going one day into a bookseller's shop in
Fleet Street to ask for the Review ; and on my expressing
my opinion to a young Scotchman, who stood behind the
counter, that Mr. Cobbett might hit as hard in his reply,
the North Briton said with some alarm—'But you don't
think, Sir, Mr. Cobbett will be able to injure the Scottish
nation ? ' I said I could not speak to that point, but
I thought he was very well able to defend himself. He 30
however did not, but has borne a grudge to the Edinburgh
Review ever since, which he hates worse than the Quarterly.
I cannot say I do.

Mr. Cobbett speaks almost as well as he writes. The
only time I ever saw him he seemed to me a very pleasant

man : easy of access, affable, clear-headed, simple and mild
in his manner, deliberate and unruffled in his speech, though
some of his expressions were not very qualified. His figure
is tall and portly : he has a good sensible face, rather full,
with little grey eyes, a hard, square forehead, a ruddy
complexion, with hair grey or powdered : and had on
a scarlet broad-cloth waistcoat, with the flaps of the
pockets hanging down, as was the custom for gentleman-
farmers in the last century, or as we see it in the pictures of
10 Members of Parliament in the reign of George I.   I certainly
did not think less favourably of him for seeing him.

From C A R L Y L E' S Essay on Scott

(First published in *The London and Westminster Review*, No. 12, 1838.)

THE healthy man is a most meritorious product of Nature,
so far as he goes. A healthy body is good ; but a soul in
right health,—it is the thing beyond all others to be prayed
for ; the blessedest thing this earth receives of Heaven.
Without artificial medicament of philosophy, or tight-lacing
of creeds (always very questionable), the healthy soul discerns what is good, and adheres to it, and retains it ;
discerns what is bad, and spontaneously casts it off.   An
20 instinct from Nature herself, like that which guides the
wild animals of the forest to their food, shews him what he
shall do, what he shall abstain from.   The false and foreign
will not adhere to him ; cant and all fantastic diseased
incrustations are impossible ;—as Walker the *Original*, in
such eminence of health was *he* for his part, *could* not, by
much abstinence from soap and water, attain to a dirty
face ! This thing thou canst work with and profit by, this
thing is substantial and worthy ; that other thing thou
canst not work with, it is trivial and inapt : so speaks
30 unerringly the inward monition of the man's whole nature.

No need of logic to prove the most argumentative absurdity absurd ; as Goethe says of himself, ' all this ran down from me like water from a man in wax-cloth dress.' Blessed is the healthy nature ; it is the coherent, sweetly cooperative, not incoherent, self-distracting, self-destructive one ! In the harmonious adjustment and play of all the faculties, the just balance of oneself gives a just feeling towards all men and all things. Glad light from within radiates outwards, and enlightens and embellishes.

Now all this can be predicated of Walter Scott, and of no British literary man that we remember in these days, to any such extent,—if it be not perhaps of one, the most opposite imaginable to Scott, but his equal in this quality and what holds of it : William Cobbett ! Nay, there are other similarities, widely different as they two look ; nor be the comparison disparaging to Scott : for Cobbett also, as the pattern John Bull of his century, strong as the rhinoceros, and with singular humanities and genialities shining through his thick skin, is a most brave phenomenon. So bounteous was Nature to us ; in the sickliest of recorded ages, when British Literature lay all puking and sprawling in Werterism, Byronism, and other Sentimentalism tearful or spasmodic (fruit of internal *wind*), Nature was kind enough to send us two healthy Men, of whom she might still say, not without pride, ' These also were made in England ; such limbs do I still make there ! ' It is one of the cheerfullest sights, let the question of its greatness be settled as you will. A healthy nature may or may not be great ; but there is no great nature that is not healthy.

From Sir HENRY LYTTON BULWER'S
Historical Characters 1868

HE left a gap in the public mind which no one else could
fill, or attempt to fill up, for his loss was not merely that of
a man, but of a habit—of a dose of strong drink which all
of us had been taking for years, most of us during our lives,
and which it was impossible for anyone again to concoct
so strongly, so strangely, with so much spice and flavour,
or with such a variety of ingredients. And there was this
peculiarity in the general regret—it extended to all persons.
Whatever a man's talents, whatever a man's opinions, he
10 sought the *Register* on the day of its appearance with eager-
ness, and read it with amusement, partly, perhaps, if
De Rochefoucault is right, because, whatever his party, he
was sure to see his friends abused. But partly also because
he was certain to find, amidst a great many lies and
abundance of impudence, some felicitous nickname, some
excellent piece of practical-looking argument, some capital
expressions, and very often some marvellously fine writing,
all the finer for being carelessly fine, and exhibiting whatever figure or sentiment it set forth in the simplest as well
20 as the most striking dress. Cobbett himself indeed said
that '*his popularity was owing to his giving truth in clear
language*'; and his language always did leave his meaning
as visible as the most limpid stream leaves its bed. But
as to its portraying truth, that is a different matter, and
would be utterly impossible unless truth has at least as
many heads as the Hydra of fable; in which case our
author may claim the merit of having portrayed them all.

This, however, is to be remarked. He rarely abused that
which was falling or fallen, but generally that which was
30 rising or uppermost. . . His praise or censure afforded a sort
of test to be taken in an inverse sense of the world's
opinion. He could not bear superiority of any kind, or

reconcile himself to its presence. As for absurdity, nothing
was too absurd for him coolly and deliberately to assert.
'There would have been no national debt and no paupers
if there had been no Reformation.'   'The population of
England had not increased one single soul since he was
born.'

Neither did his coarseness know any bounds. He called
a newspaper a cut-and-thrust weapon, to be used without
any mercy or delicacy, and never thought of anything but
how he could strike the hardest. 'Bark away, hell-hounds, 10
till you are suffocated in your own foam.' 'This hatter
turned painter [Samuel F. Bradford], whose heart is as
black and as foul as the liquid in which he dabbles.' . . .
His mode of commencing an attack also was often singularly
effective from its humour and personality: ' He was a sly-
looking fellow, with a hard, slate-coloured countenance.
He set out by blushing, and I may leave any one to guess
at the efforts that must be made to get a blush through
a skin like his.' 'And now, having settled the point in
question, give me leave to ask, my sweet sleepy-eyed Sir.'. . . 20
His writing was often what the gentlemen of the United
States call ' stump-speaking.' . . . His talents for fastening
his claws into anything or anyone by a word or an expression
and holding them down to scorn or up to horror was un-
rivalled. ' Prosperity Robinson ', ' Œolus Canning ', ' the
pink-nosed Liverpool ', the ' unbaptised buttonless black-
guards ' (by which he designated the followers of Penn)
were expressions with which he attached ridicule where
he could not fix reproach, and it is said that nothing was
so teasing to Lord Erskine as being constantly addressed 30
by his second title of ' Baron Clackmannan.'. . .

It must be added in his praise that he is always a hearty
Englishman. He may vary in his opinions as to doctrines
and as to men, but he is ever for making England great,
powerful, and prosperous—her people healthy, brave, and

free. He never falls into the error of mistaking political economy for the whole of political science. He does not say, ' Be wealthy, make money, and care about nothing else '. He advocates rural pursuits as invigorating to a population, although less profitable than manufacturing. He desires to see Englishmen fit for war as well as for peace. There is none of that puling primness about him which marks the philosophers who would have a great nation, like a good boy at a private school, fit for nothing but obedience and books.

This very spirit of combativeness is the spirit of journalism ; and Cobbett was not only this spirit embodied, but — and this renders his life so remarkable in our history—he represented journalism, and fought the fight of journalism against authority, when it was still a doubt which would gain the day.

Let us not forget that blind and uncalculating intolerance with which the law struggled against opinion from 1809 to 1822. Writers during this period were transported, imprisoned, and fined without limit or conscience ; and just when Government became more lenient to legitimate newspapers, it engaged in a new conflict with unstamped ones. No less than 500 vendors of these were imprisoned within six years. The contest was one of life and death. Amidst the general din of the battle was heard Cobbett's bold, bitter, scornful voice, cheering on the small but determined band, which defied tyranny without employing force. The failure of the last prosecution against the *Register* was the general failure of prosecutions against the Press, and may be said to have closed the contest, in which Government lost power every time that it made victims.

From THOROLD ROGERS'S
Historical Gleanings, 1869

As a controversialist, Cobbett was constantly unfair from his vindictive violence. Men who have been persecuted are rarely tolerant ; the most patient martyr has often been the most savage inquisitor. Cobbett felt himself wounded, and he retaliated with ferocious energy. ' He had,' says Hazlitt, ' the back trick simply the best of any man in Illyria '. He never hesitated in his revenge, and he continued it after revenge was indecent, as well as superfluous. He hated Castlereagh—most of Castlereagh's opponents had reason to hate him—during his life, and he gloated over the circumstances of Castlereagh's suicide after his death. Canning felt the blows of his bludgeon, for Canning, like most satirists, was sensitive. Lord Lytton calls Cobbett ' the contentious man ' ; but the adjective, though eminently suggestive, hardly covers the range of this writer's controversial nature. He was vindictive, with the greatest facility of retaliation. Some men, like Wilkes, are irresistible in repartee ; others, like Canning, have a vein of polished irony ; some, like Moore, have a gay wit, which pleases even when it stings the most, and is hardly offensive to its object : but Cobbett was capable of that harsh ridicule which springs from an unforgiving nature, and is unforgiven ;—which bruises instead of wounding ; but which roused in its day whole masses of the people to band themselves against what they were taught to believe was wrong or selfishness.

It may seem to most of my hearers that the politician is more prominent in Cobbett than the economist. I have, it is to be admitted, given greater prominence to the former constituent in the career of this remarkable man ; but, in truth, the substratum of all Cobbett's positive convictions was economical. He never swerved from his purpose,—

that of undertaking the defence of the farmer and the peasant. As a consequence, his influence was exceedingly great among the class from whom he sprung. . . .

In one of his latest works he tells us that, at Charlbury in Oxfordshire, every man who had been a farmer thirty years before was on the poor-book in 1835. He witnessed, with wondering indignation, the gradual decline of the class which he loved, and to which he belonged by birth. He did not, however, see how distinctly traceable this fact was
10 to the system of precarious tenure, of artificial legislation, and thereupon of perpetual and damaging fluctuations in the price of the agricultural staple. It may be the case, as some economists think, that the large system of cultivation is better suited to the conditions under which high farming is carried on than small cultivation can be. The hypothesis is at least doubtful. But there is no doubt that this large system has destroyed the yeomanry and degraded the peasantry of England. It is equally certain that the change has not been induced as a consequence of
20 the economical principles with which it is supposed to be in harmony ; but in absolute defiance of them.

The condition of the peasant is now lower than it was even in Cobbett's time. In the days of Arthur Young, the agricultural labourer was far better off than he is now. You who live in the centre of active industries, and among whom, therefore, the rate of wages in rural districts is heightened by the competition of manufacturing energy, have probably no conception of the stolid misery which is the unvarying lot of the farm labourer in the South of
30 England. His wages have scarcely risen for the last twenty years. A few of his luxuries have been cheapened. Most of the necessaries of his humble life have been made dearer (for the development of railway communication has equalized prices in town and country), if indeed they are not, owing to the regularity of the market, cheaper in the

former than in the latter. The prices of meat, butter, cheese, and milk, are at present double those at which they stood twenty years ago in rural districts. The rate of house-rent too has increased, and will it seems increase, owing to causes on which I have no time to dwell now. The best proof of the depth to which the south-country hind has descended, is to be seen in the formation of children's gangs, and in the increasingly early age at which children labour.

Cobbett, during the great war, and the reaction which followed upon peace, saw the beginning of this misery. He traced it, in some degree, to its true causes, the absorption of capital in the war, and the limited demand for labour. The wealth of the country, Cobbett thought, with some reason, was consumed in foreign expenditure, in foreign subsidies, and, in no small degree, in the profits of loan-mongers. Upon the latter functionaries he looked with intense disfavour.

Like most men of warm sympathies and warmer hatreds, Cobbett believed in the possibility of remedying these evils by communistic expedients. His ' History of the Reformation ' was an attack on the hereditary wealth of the Tudor nobles. His ' Legacy to Parsons ' was an assault on the endowments of the Church. His quarrels with O'Connell, his abuse of Malthus, Mr. Lowe of Bingham, and Mr. Chadwick, were the fruit of his admiration of the old poor law.

The poor law of Elizabeth was not a compensation for the loss which the people sustained by the suppression of the monasteries and the alienation of their estates. But it was a consequence of this great social change. The wealth of these orders was rapidly dissipated by Henry VIII. The price which his courtiers and grantees paid for their possessions was as rapidly squandered. Upon this waste of public capital, came the debasement of the currency, to which I have already alluded. Agriculture was abandoned

and sheep-farming substituted in its place. The peasantry was unemployed and starving. Vagrancy was made a capital offence, but ineffectually. At last a poor law was the only refuge from brigandage. Pauperism, which hardly existed during the prosperous epoch of the eighteenth century, became the prominent evil of the nineteenth. In some parishes, every shilling of rent was absorbed in the relief of the poor. It was necessary that this system should be checked, and that the remedy, however sharp it
10 might be, should be found and applied.

Malthus and the writers of his school advocated the most extreme processes. Cobbett thought that, granting the present appropriation of the soil, and allowing that the usurpation of the landowner, as he conceived it, should be undisturbed, the poor had an inalienable right to maintenance from land. 'The right to land', said he, 'is founded in labour, and in labour only'. Labour is divorced from the land, but it cannot be defrauded of its interest in the distribution of that which it alone has
20 earned. To him, therefore, the argument of these economists was not merely distasteful, but their plans were immoral and fraudulent. It was not the poor law, he thought, which had degraded the labourer, but misgovernment and reckless expenditure. It was not an attempt to better his condition by wholesome severity, which Malthus and Lowe advocated, but the relief of the landlord's rent, and the saving of the parson's tithes.

Fortunately, Cobbett and those who reasoned with him were foiled. Workhouses are no longer the warrens in
30 which hereditary paupers are bred and brought up, but penitentiaries to the able-bodied, refuges for the aged and sick. It is true that the issue of the workhouse system is not tried by its success in discouraging the relief of capable workmen by means of a public charity. The question is yet unsettled, whether or no the agricultural labourer is

not entitled to some compensation as a set-off to those laws and customs which have annihilated his interest in the soil ; but no one in these days doubts that, whatever that compensation should be, it cannot and should not be a system which wholly destroys any restraint of prudence, every impulse of self-reliance and independence. . .

It would carry me far beyond the limits which time imposes on an evening lecture, if I were to attempt a fuller sketch of England at the day of Cobbett's death, and England in our own immediate present. It is sufficient to say, that though some interests have suffered—those, unhappily, which needed elevation the most,—the material progress of the country has on the whole been rapid and continuous. Prosperity has followed on wise legislation, for it is an axiom in politics that the wage-earning classes have a far greater interest in wise government and public morality than their wealthier fellow-countrymen. The sinister predictions which accompanied the reforms of the last forty years have been falsified, and would be forgotten, were they not invariably resuscitated when other changes are demanded and impending. And above all, the United Kingdom has been fruitful in brave and wise men, whose public life has stood out in marked contrast to the churchmen and statesmen of Cobbett's stormy retrospect.

Again, it is not easy to discover what are the special influences which the career of such a man exerted over the age in which he lived, and over that which succeeded it. It was impossible that a popular writer, who played so notable a part on the public stage, should fail of aiding the forces out of which society has grown to its present stature and form. At least, Cobbett familiarised the people with the most effective kind of popular education, that, namely, which criticises public events and public characters. If he was not the progenitor of the free press, he was at least one of its eldest sons. It is true that he disfigured his

vigorous English by personalities, and injured his own
reputation by his unreasoning and ferocious animosities,
but he had a hearty love for his country and his countrymen,
and a readiness to strive for what he believed to be the
right.   For no popularity can be enduring which does not
lay its foundations in a real interest for the public good,
though the means may be taken in error, and the effect
marred by lack of experience.   In Cobbett's nature the
good preponderated vastly over the evil.   The influence of
10 his writings was on the whole beneficent.   His many
blemishes, both of mind and temper, prevented him from
being great.   The faults of his education led him into many
a hasty judgment.   But he kept alive much that was true
and just in an age when truth and justice were reduced
to struggle for existence.   We may be sure that there was
much that is worthy in a man whose writings were read
by millions during his life, and whose coffin was followed
by thousands when he was laid in the sepulchre of his
fathers.

PERSONAL REMINISCENCES

By Hazlitt

From *Conversations of James Northcote*, 1830; first published in
The Atlas, April 26, 1829.

20   *Northcote.*   Though you do not know Sir Walter Scott,
I think I have heard you say you have seen him ?

Hazlitt.   Yes ; he put me in mind of Cobbett, with his
florid face and scarlet gown, which were just like the
other's red face and scarlet waistcoat.   The one is like an
English farmer, the other like a Scotch laird.   Both are
large, robust men with great strength and composure of
features ; but I saw nothing of the *ideal* character in the

romance-writer any more than I looked for it in the politician.

Northcote. Indeed ! But you have a vast opinion of Cobbett too, haven't you ? Oh, he's a giant ! He has such prodigious strength ; he tears up a subject by the roots. Did you ever read his grammar or see his attack on Mrs. ——— ? It was like a hawk pouncing on a wren. I should be terribly afraid to get into his hands. And then his homely familiar way of writing—it is not from necessity or vulgarity, but to show his contempt for aristocratic pride and arrogance. He only has a kitchen-garden ; he could have a flower-garden too, if he chose. Peter Pindar said his style was like the Horse Guards, only one storey above the ground, while Junius's had all the airy elegance of Whitehall : but he could raise his style just as high as he pleased, though he does not want to sacrifice strength to elegance. He knows better what he is about.

By George Gilfillan

From *A Second Gallery of Literary Portraits,* 1850.

THOSE who expected to find in Cobbett a rude truculent barbarian, were disappointed. They found, instead, a tall, stout, mild-faced, broad-shouldered, farmer-looking man, with a spice of humour lurking in his eye, but without one vestige of fierceness or malignity either in his look or demeanour. His private manners were simple, unaffected —almost gentlemanly. His mode of addressing an audience was quiet, clear, distinct, and conversational ; and the fury and the fervour of the demagogue alike were wanting. The most sarcastic and provoking things oozed out at his lips like milk or honey. Add to this, perfect self-possession, his usual vein of humour somewhat subdued into keeping with his audience, and a certain cajolery in his manner, as the most notable features in his mode of public address. . . .

By Mary Russell Mitford

From *Recollections of a Literary Life*, 1852.

HE had at that time a large house at Botley, with
a lawn and gardens sweeping down to the Bursledon River,
which divided his (Mr. Cobbett's) territories from the
beautiful grounds of the old friend, where we had been
originally staying, the great squire of the place. His own
house—large, high, massive, red, and square, and perched
on a considerable eminence—always struck me as being not
unlike its proprietor. . . I never saw hospitality more
genuine, more simple, or more thoroughly successful in
10 the great end of hospitality, the putting of everybody
completely at ease. There was not the slightest attempt at
finery, or display, or gentility. They called it a farmhouse,
and everything was in accordance with the largest idea
of a great English yeoman of the old time. Everything was
excellent, everything abundant—all served with the greatest
nicety by trim waiting-damsels : and everything went on
with such quiet regularity, that of the large circle of guests
not one could find himself in the way. I need not say
a word more in praise of the good wife . . . to whom this
20 admirable order was mainly due. She was a sweet motherly
woman, realising our notion of one of Scott's most charming
characters, *Ailie Dinmont*, in her simplicity, her kindness,
and her devotion to her husband and her children.

At this time William Cobbett was at the height of his
political reputation ; but of politics we heard little, and
should, I think, have heard nothing, but for an occasional
red-hot patriot, who would introduce the subject, which
our host would fain put aside and got rid of as soon as
possible. There was something of *Dandie Dinmont* about
30 him, with his unfailing good humour and good spirits—
his heartiness, his love of field sports, and his liking for

a foray. He was a tall, stout man, fair, and sunburnt, with a bright smile, and an air compounded of the soldier and the farmer, to which his habit of wearing an eternal red waistcoat contributed not a little. He was, I think, the most athletic and vigorous person that I have ever known. Nothing could tire him. At home in the morning he would begin by mowing his own lawn, beating his gardener, Robinson, the best mower, except himself, in the parish at that fatiguing work.

For early rising indeed he had an absolute passion, and some of the poetry that we trace in his writings, whenever he speaks of scenery or of rural objects, broke out in his method of training his children into his own matutinal habits. The boy who was first down stairs was called the Lark for the day, and had, amongst other indulgences, the pretty privilege of making his mother's nosegay and that of any lady visitors. Nor was this the only trace of poetical feeling that he displayed. Whenever he described a place, were it only to say where such a covey lay, or such a hare was found sitting, you could see it, so graphic—so vivid— so true was the picture. He showed the same taste in the purchase of his beautiful farm at Botley, Fairthorn ; even in the pretty name. To be sure, he did not give the name, but I always thought that it unconsciously influenced his choice in the purchase. The beauty of the situation certainly did. The fields lay along the Bursledon River, and might have been shown to a foreigner as a specimen of the richest and loveliest English scenery.

From EBENEZER ELLIOTT'S

Elegy on William Cobbett

Oh, bear him where the rain can fall,
  And where the winds can blow,
And let the sun weep o'er his pall
  As to the grave ye go !

And in some little lone churchyard
  Beside the growing corn,
Lay gentle nature's stern prose bard,
  Her mightiest—peasant-born.

Yes ! Let the wild-flower wed his grave,
  That bees may murmur near,
When o'er his last home bend the brave,
  And say—' A man lies here '.

Selections from
COBBETT

FROM THE STORY OF HIS LIFE

Childhood and Youth

(From *The Life and Adventures of Peter Porcupine*, August 1796.)

To be descended from an illustrious family certainly reflects honour on any man, in spite of the sans-culotte principles of the present day. This is, however, an honour that I have no pretension to. All that I can boast of in my birth is that I was born in Old England ; the country from whence came the men who explored and settled North America ; the country of Penn, and of all those to whom this country is indebted.

With respect to my ancestors, I shall go no further back 10 than my grandfather, and for this plain reason, that I never heard talk of any prior to him. He was a day-labourer ; and I have heard my father say, that he worked for one farmer from the day of his marriage to that of his death, upwards of forty years. He died before I was born, but I have often slept beneath the same roof that had sheltered him, and where his widow dwelt for several years after his death. It was a little thatched cottage, with a garden before the door. It had but two windows ; a damson tree shaded one, and a clump of filberts the other. 20 Here I and my brothers went every Christmas and Whitsuntide to spend a week or two, and torment the poor old woman with our noise and dilapidations. She used to give us milk and bread for breakfast, an apple pudding for our dinner, and a piece of bread and cheese for supper. Her fire was made of turf, cut from the neighbouring heath, and her evening light was a rush dipped in grease.

How much better is it, thus to tell the naked truth,

than to descend to such miserable shifts as Doctor Franklin has had recourse to, in order to persuade people that his forefathers were men of wealth and consideration. Not being able to refer his reader to the herald's office for proofs of the fame and antiquity of his family, he appeals to the etymology of his name, and points out a passage in an obsolete book, whence he has the conscience to insist on our concluding, that, in the Old English language, a *Franklin* meant a man of *good reputation and of consequence*. According to Dr. Johnson, a Franklin was what we now call a gentleman's steward or land-bailiff, a personage one degree above a bumbailiff, and that's all.

Every one will, I hope, have the goodness to believe, that my grandfather was no philosopher. Indeed he was not. He never made a lightning-rod, nor bottled up a single quart of sun-shine, in the whole course of his life. He was no almanack-maker, nor quack, nor chimney-doctor, nor soap-boiler, nor ambassador, nor printer's devil : neither was he a deist, and all his children were born in wedlock. The legacies he left, were, his scythe, his reap-hook, and his flail ; he bequeathed no old and irrecoverable debts to an hospital : he never *cheated the poor during his life*, nor *mocked them in his death*. He has, it is true, been suffered to sleep quietly beneath the green sord ; but, if his descendants cannot point to his statue over the door of a library, they have not the mortification to hear him daily accused of having been a whoremaster, a hypocrite, and an infidel.

My father, when I was born, was a farmer. The reader will easily believe, from the poverty of his parents, that he had received no very brilliant education : he was, however, learned, for a man in his rank of life. When a little boy, he drove plough for two-pence a day ; and these his earnings, were appropriated to the expenses of an evening school. What a village schoolmaster could be expected to

teach, he had learnt ; and had, besides, considerably im-
proved himself, in several branches of the mathematics.
He understood land-surveying well, and was often chosen
to draw the plans of disputed territory : in short, he had
the reputation of possessing experience and understanding,
which never fails, in England, to give a man in a country
place, some little weight with his neighbours. He was
honest, industrious, and frugal ; it was not, therefore,
wonderful, that he should be situated in a good farm, and
10 happy in a wife of his own rank, like him, beloved and
respected.

So much for my ancestors, from whom, if I derive no
honour, I derive no shame.

I had (and I hope I yet have) three brothers : the eldest
is a shopkeeper ; the second a farmer, and the youngest,
if alive, is in the service of the Honourable East India
Company, a private soldier, perhaps, as I have been, in the
service of the king. I was born on the ninth of March,
1766 : the exact age of my brothers, I have forgotten ;
20 but I remember having heard my mother say, that there
was but three years and three quarters difference between
the age of the oldest and that of the youngest.

A father like ours, it will be readily supposed, did not
suffer us to eat the bread of idleness. I do not remember
the time when I did not earn my living. My first occupa-
tion was, driving the small birds from the turnip-seed, and
the rooks from the peas. When I first trudged a-field, with
my wooden bottle and my satchel swung over my shoulders,
I was hardly able to climb the gates and stiles ; and, at
30 the close of the day, to reach home was a task of infinite
difficulty. My next employment was weeding wheat, and
leading a single horse at harrowing barley. Hoeing peas
followed, and hence I arrived at the honour of joining the
reapers in harvest, driving the team, and holding plough.
We were all of us strong and laborious, and my father used to

boast that he had four boys, the eldest of whom was but fifteen years old, who did as much work as any three men in the parish of Farnham. Honest pride, and happy days !

I have some faint recollection of going to school to an old woman, who, I believe, did not succeed in learning me my letters. In the winter evenings my father learnt us all to read and write, and gave us a pretty tolerable knowledge of arithmetic. Grammar he did not perfectly understand himself, and therefore his endeavours to learn us that necessarily failed ; for, though he thought he understood it, and though he made us get the rules by heart, we learnt nothing at all of the principles.

Our religion was that of the Church of England, to which I have ever remained attached ; the more so, perhaps, as it bears the name of my country. As my ancestors were never persecuted for their religious opinions, they never had an opportunity of giving such a singular proof of their faith as Doctor Franklin's grandfather did, when he kept his Bible under the lid of a close-stool. (What a book-case !) If I had been in the place of Doctor Franklin, I never would have related this ridiculous circumstance, especially as it must be construed into a boast of his grandfather's having an extraordinary degree of veneration for a book, which, it is well known, he himself *durst* not believe in.

As to politics, we were like the rest of the country people in England ; that is to say, we neither knew nor thought any thing about the matter. The shouts of victory, or the murmurs at a defeat, would now-and-then break in upon our tranquillity for a moment ; but I do not remember ever having seen a newspaper in the house ; and, most certainly, that privation did not render us less industrious, happy, or free.

After, however, the American war had continued for some time, and the cause and nature of it began to be understood, or rather misunderstood, by the lower classes

of the people in England, we became a little better acquainted with subjects of this kind. It is well known that
the people were, as to numbers, nearly equally divided in
their opinions concerning that war and their wishes
respecting the result of it. My father was a partizan of
the Americans : he used frequently to dispute on the
subject with the gardener of a nobleman who lived near
us. This was generally done with good humour, over a pot
of our best ale ; yet the disputants sometimes grew warm,
10 and gave way to language that could not fail to attract
our attention. My father was worsted, without doubt, as
he had for antagonist a shrewd and sensible old Scotchman,
far his superior in political knowledge ; but he pleaded
before a partial audience : we thought there was but one
wise man in the world, and that that one was our father.
He who pleaded the cause of the Americans had an
advantage, too, with young minds : he had only to
represent the king's troops as sent to cut the throats of
a people, our friends and relations, merely because they
20 would not submit to oppression ; and his cause was gained.
Speaking to the passions is ever sure to succeed on the
uninformed.

Men of integrity are generally pretty obstinate, in
adhering to an opinion once adopted. Whether it was
owing to this, or to the weakness of Mr. Martin's arguments,
I will not pretend to say ; but he never could make a con-
vert of my father : he continued an American, and so
staunch a one that he would not have suffered his best
friend to drink success to the king's arms at his table.
30 I cannot give the reader a better idea of his obstinacy in
this respect, and of the length to which this difference in
sentiment was carried in England, than by relating the
following instance.

My father used to take one of us with him every year
to the great hop-fair at Wey-Hill. The fair was held at

Old-Michaelmas-tide, and the journey was, to us, a sort of reward for the labours of the summer. It happened to be my turn to go thither the very year that Long-Island was taken by the British. A great company of hop-merchants and farmers were just sitting down to supper as the post arrived, bringing in the Extraordinary Gazette, which announced the victory. A hop-factor from London took the paper, placed his chair upon the table, and began to read with an audible voice. He was opposed, a dispute ensued, and my father retired, taking me by the hand, to 10 another apartment, where we supped with about a dozen others of the same sentiments. Here Washington's health, and success to the Americans, were repeatedly toasted, and this was the first time, as far as I can recollect, that I ever heard the General's name mentioned. Little did I then dream that I should ever see the man, and still less that I should hear some of his own countrymen reviling and execrating him.

Let not the reader imagine that I wish to assume any merit from this mistaken prejudice of an honoured and 20 beloved parent. Whether he was right or wrong is not now worth talking about : that I had no opinion of my own is certain ; for, had my father been on the other side, I should have been on the other side too ; and should have looked upon the company I then made a part of as malcontents and rebels. I mention these circumstances merely to show that I was not ' nursed in the lap of aristocracy,' and that I did not imbibe my principles, or prejudices, from those who were the advocates of blind submission. If my father had any fault, it was not being submissive enough, 30 and I am much afraid my acquaintance have but too often discovered the same fault in his son.

It would be as useless as unentertaining to dwell on the occupations and sports of a country boy ; to lead the reader to fairs, cricket-matches, and hare-hunts. I shall

therefore come at once to the epoch when an accident
happened that gave that turn to my future life which at
last brought me to the United States.

Towards the autumn of 1782 I went to visit a relation
who lived in the neighbourhood of Portsmouth. From the
top of Portsdown I, for the first time, beheld the sea, and
no sooner did I behold it than I wished to be a sailor.
I could never account for this sudden impulse, nor can
I now. Almost all English boys feel the same inclination :
10 it would seem that, like young ducks, instinct leads them
to rush on the bosom of the water.

But it was not the sea alone that I saw : the grand fleet
was riding at anchor at Spithead. I had heard of the
wooden walls of Old England : I had formed my ideas of
a ship and of a fleet ; but what I now beheld so far
surpassed what I had ever been able to form a conception
of that I stood lost between astonishment and admiration.
I had heard talk of the glorious deeds of our Admirals and
sailors, of the defeat of the Spanish Armada, and of all
20 those memorable combats that good and true Englishmen
never fail to relate to their children about a hundred times
a year. The brave Rodney's victories over our natural
enemies, the French and Spaniards, had long been the
theme of our praise, and the burden of our songs. The
sight of the fleet brought all these into my mind ; in
confused order, it is true, but with irresistible force. My
heart was inflated with national pride. The sailors were
my countrymen ; the fleet belonged to my country, and
surely I had my part in it, and in all its honours : yet,
30 these honours I had not earned ; I took to myself a sort
of reproach for possessing what I had no right to, and
resolved to have a just claim by sharing in the hardships
and dangers.

I arrived at my uncle's late in the evening with my
mind full of my sea-faring project. Though I had walked

thirty miles during the day, and consequently was well
wearied, I slept not a moment. It was no sooner day-
light, than I arose and walked down towards the old castle,
on the beach of Spithead. For a sixpence given to an
invalid, I got permission to go upon the battlements :
here I had a closer view of the fleet, and at every look my
impatience to be on board increased. In short, I went
from the castle to Portsmouth, got into a boat, and was
in a few minutes on board the Pegasus, man of war.

The Captain had more compassion than is generally met 10
with in men of his profession : he represented to me the
toils I must undergo, and the punishment that the least
disobedience or neglect would subject me to. He persuaded
me to return home, and I remember he concluded his
advice, with telling me that it was better to be led to
church in a halter, to be tied to a girl that I did not like,
than to be tied to the gang-way, or, as the sailors call it,
married to *Miss Roper*. From the conclusion of this wholesome counsel I perceived that the captain thought I had
eloped on account of a bastard. I blushed, and that con- 20
firmed him in his opinion ; but I declare to the reader that
I was no more guilty of such an offence than Mr. Swanwick,
or any other gentleman who is constitutionally virtuous.
No ; thank heaven, I have none of the Franklintonian
crimes to accuse myself of ; my children do not hang their
hats up in other men's houses ; I am neither patriot nor
philosopher.

I in vain attempted to convince Captain Berkley, that
choice alone had led me to the sea ; he sent me on shore,
and I at last quitted Portsmouth ; but not before I had 30
applied to the Port-Admiral, Evans, to get my name enrolled among those who were destined for the service.
I was, in some sort, obliged to acquaint the Admiral with
what had passed on board the Pegasus, in consequence of
which my request was refused, and I happily escaped,

sorely against my will, from the most toilsome and perilous
profession in the world.

I returned once more to the plough, but I was spoiled for
a farmer. I had, before my Portsmouth adventure, never
known any other ambition than that of surpassing my
brothers in the different labours of the field ; but it was
quite otherwise now ; I sighed for a sight of the world ;
the little island of Britain, seemed too small a compass for
me. The things in which I had taken the most delight
10 were neglected ; the singing of the birds grew insipid, and
even the heart-cheering cry of the hounds, after which
I formerly used to fly from my work, bound o'er the fields,
and dash through the brakes and coppices, was heard with
the most torpid indifference. Still, however, I remained at
home till the following spring, when I quitted it, perhaps
for ever.

It was on the sixth of May 1783 that I, like Don Quixote,
sallied forth to seek adventures. I was dressed in my
holiday clothes, in order to accompany two or three lasses
20 to Guildford fair. They were to assemble at a house
about three miles from my home, where I was to attend
them ; but, unfortunately for me, I had to cross the
London turnpike road. The stage coach had just turned
the summit of a hill, and was rattling down towards me
at a merry rate. The notion of going to London never
entered my mind till this very moment, yet the step was
completely determined on before the coach came to the
spot where I stood. Up I got, and was in London about
nine o'clock in the evening.

30   It was by mere accident that I had money enough to
defray the expenses of this day. Being rigged out for the
fair, I had three or four crown and half crown pieces,
(which most certainly I did not intend to spend), besides
a few shillings and half pence. This, my little all, which
I had been years in amassing, melted away, like snow

before the sun, when touched by the fingers of the innkeepers and their waiters.   In short, when I arrived at
Ludgate Hill, and had paid my fare, I had but about half
a crown in my pocket.

By a commencement of that good luck which has hitherto
attended me, through all the situations in which fortune
has placed me, I was preserved from ruin.   A gentleman,
who was one of the passengers in the stage, fell into conversation with me at dinner, and he soon learnt that I was
going, I knew not whither, nor for what.   This gentleman 10
was a hop merchant in the borough of Southwark, and,
upon closer inquiry, it appeared that he had often dealt
with my father at Wey-Hill.   He knew the danger I was
in ; he was himself a father, and he felt for my parents.
His house became my home ; he wrote to my father, and
endeavoured to prevail on me to obey his orders, which
were to return immediately home.   I am ashamed to say
that I was disobedient.   It was the first time I had ever
been so, and I have repented of it from that moment to
this.   Willingly would I have returned ; but pride would 20
not suffer me to do it.   I feared the scoffs of my acquaint-
ances more than the real evils that threatened me.

My generous preserver, finding my obstinacy not to be
overcome, began to look out for an employment for me.
He was preparing an advertisement for the newspaper,
when an acquaintance of his, an attorney, called in to see
him.   He related my adventure to this gentleman, whose
name was Holland, and who, happening to want an under
strapping quill-driver, did me the honour to take me into
his service, and the next day saw me perched upon a great 30
high stool in an obscure chamber in Gray's Inn, endeavouring to decipher the crabbed draughts of my employer.

I could write a good plain hand, but I could not read the
pot-hooks and hangers of Mr. Holland.   He was a month
in learning me to copy without almost continual assistance,

and even then I was of but little use to him ; for, besides
that I wrote a snail's pace, my want of knowledge in
orthography gave him infinite trouble : so that, for the
first two months, I was a dead weight upon his hands.
Time, however, rendered me useful ; and Mr. Holland was
pleased to tell me that he was very well satisfied with me,
just at the very moment when I began to grow extremely
dissatisfied with him.

No part of my life has been totally unattended with
10 pleasure, except the eight or nine months I passed in
Gray's Inn. The office (for so the dungeon where I wrote
was called) was so dark that, on cloudy days, we were
obliged to burn candle. I worked like a galley-slave from
five in the morning till eight or nine at night, and sometimes all night long. How many quarrels have I assisted
to foment and perpetuate between those poor innocent
fellows, John Doe and Richard Roe ! How many times
(God forgive me !) have I sent them to assault each other
with guns, swords, staves and pitch-forks, and then brought
20 them to answer for their misdeeds before our Sovereign
Lord the King seated in His Court of Westminster ! When
I think of the *saids* and *soforths*, and the counts of tautology
that I scribbled over ; when I think of those sheets of
seventy-two words, and those lines two inches a part, my
brain turns. Gracious heaven ! if I am doomed to be
wretched, bury me beneath Iceland snows, and let me feed
on blubber ; stretch me under the burning line, and deny
me thy propitious dews ; nay, if it be thy will, suffocate me
with the infected and pestilential air of a democratic club-
30 room ; but save me from the desk of an attorney !

Mr. Holland was but little in the chambers himself.
He always went out to dinner, while I was left to be
provided for by the *laundress*, as he called her. Those
gentlemen of the law who have resided in the Inns of
Court in London know very well what a *laundress* means.

Ours was, I believe, the oldest and ugliest of the sisterhood.
She had age and experience enough to be Lady Abbess of
all the nuns in all the convents of Irish-Town. It would
be wronging the witch of Endor to compare her to this
hag, who was the only creature that deigned to enter into
conversation with me. All except the name, I was in
prison, and this weird sister was my keeper. Our chambers
were, to me, what the subterraneous cavern was to Gil
Blas : his description of the Dame Leonarda exactly suited
my laundress ; nor were the professions, or rather the
practice, of our masters altogether dissimilar.

I never quitted this gloomy recess except on Sundays,
when I usually took a walk to St. James's Park, to feast
my eyes with the sight of the trees, the grass, and the
water. In one of these walks I happened to cast my eye
on an advertisement, inviting all loyal young men, who
had a mind to gain riches and glory, to repair to a certain
rendezvous, where they might enter into His Majesty's
marine service, and have the peculiar happiness and honour
of being enrolled in the Chatham Division. I was not
ignorant enough to be the dupe of this morsel of military
bombast ; but a change was what I wanted : besides,
I knew that marines went to sea, and my desire to be on
that element had rather increased than diminished by my
being penned up in London. In short, I resolved to join
this glorious corps ; and, to avoid all possibility of being
discovered by my friends, I went down to Chatham and
enlisted, into the marines as I thought, but the next
morning I found myself before a Captain of a marching
regiment. There was no retreating : I had taken a shilling
to drink his Majesty's health, and his further bounty was
ready for my reception.

When I told the Captain (who was an Irishman, and
who has since been an excellent friend to me) that I thought
myself engaged in the marines : ' By Jasus ! my lad,' said

he, ' and you have had a narrow escape.' He told me that the regiment into which I had been so happy as to enlist was one of the oldest and boldest in the whole army, and that it was at that moment serving in that fine, flourishing, and plentiful country, Nova Scotia. He dwelt long on the beauties and riches of this terrestrial paradise, and dismissed me, perfectly enchanted with the prospect of a voyage thither.

' Born and bred up in the sweet air '

(From the *Advice to Young Men*, 1829.)

BORN and bred up in the sweet air myself, I was resolved
10 that they [i. e. his children] should be bred up in it too. Enjoying rural scenes and sports, as I had done, when a boy, as much as any one that ever was born, I was resolved that they should have the same enjoyments tendered to them. When I was a very little boy, I was, in the barley-sowing season, going along by the side of a field near WAVERLEY ABBEY ; the primroses and blue-bells bespangling the banks on both sides of me ; a thousand linnets singing in a spreading oak over my head ; while the jingle of the traces and the whistling of the ploughboys
20 saluted my ear from over the hedge ; and, as it were to snatch me from the enchantment, the hounds at that instant, having started a hare in the hanger on the other side of the field, came up scampering over it in full cry, taking me after them many a mile. I was not more than eight years old ; but this particular scene has presented itself to my mind many times every year from that day to this. I always enjoy it over again ; and I was resolved to give, if possible, the same enjoyments to my children.

(From *Rural Rides*, September 27, 1822.)

WE went a little out of the way to go to a place called the *Bourn*, which lies in the heath at about a mile from Farnham. It is a winding narrow valley, down which, during the wet season of the year, there runs a stream beginning at the *Holt Forest*, and emptying itself into the *Wey* just below Moor Park, which was the seat of Sir William Temple when Swift was residing with him. We went to this bourn in order that I might show my son the spot where I received the rudiments of my education. There is a little hop-garden in which I used to work when from eight to ten years old ; from which I have scores of times run to follow the hounds, leaving the hoe to do the best it could to destroy the weeds ; but the most interesting thing was a *sand-hill*, which goes from a part of the heath down to the rivulet. As a due mixture of pleasure with toil, I, with two brothers, used occasionally to *desport* ourselves, as the lawyers call it, at this sand-hill. Our diversion was this : we used to go to the top of the hill, which was steeper than the roof of a house ; one used to draw his arms out of the sleeves of his smock-frock, and lay himself down with his arms by his sides ; and then the others, one at head and the other at feet, sent him rolling down the hill like a barrel or a log of wood. By the time he got to the bottom his hair, eyes, ears, nose, and mouth were all full of this loose sand ; then the others took their turn, and at every roll there was a monstrous spell of laughter. I had often told my sons of this while they were very little, and I now took one of them to see the spot. But that was not all. This was the spot where I was receiving my *education* ; and this was the sort of education ; and I am perfectly satisfied that if I had not received such an education, or something very much like it ; that, if I had been brought up a milksop, with a nursery-maid everlastingly at my heels, I should have been at this day as great a fool, as inefficient a mortal, as any of those frivolous idiots that are turned out from Winchester and Westminster School, or from any of those dens of dunces called colleges and universities.

(From Rural Rides, October 27, 1825.)

WE came hither by the way of Waverley Abbey and Moor Park. On the commons I showed Richard some of my old hunting scenes, when I was of his age, or younger, reminding him that I was obliged to hunt on foot. We
10 got leave to go and see the grounds at Waverley where all the old monks' garden walls are totally gone, and where the spot is become a sort of lawn. I showed him the spot where the strawberry garden was, and where I, when sent to gather *hautboys*, used to eat every remarkably fine one, instead of letting it go to be eaten by Sir Robert Rich. I showed him a tree, close by the ruins of the Abbey, from a limb of which I once fell into the river, in an attempt to take the nest of a *crow*, which had artfully placed it upon a branch so far from the trunk as not to be able to bear
20 the weight of a boy eight years old. I showed him an old elm-tree, which was hollow even then, into which I, when a very little boy, once saw a cat go, that was as big as a middle-sized spaniel dog, for relating which I got a great scolding, for standing to which I, at last, got a beating ; but stand to which I still did.

In the 54th Foot, 1784–1791

(From the *Advice to Young Men*.)

I CAN truly say, that I owe more of my great labours to my strict adherence to the precepts that I have here given you than to all the natural abilities with which I have been endowed ; for these, whatever may have been their
30 amount, would have been of comparatively little use, even

aided by great sobriety and abstinence, if I had not, in
early life, contracted the blessed habit of husbanding well
my time. To this, more than to any other thing, I owed
my very extraordinary promotion in the army.   I was
always ready : if I had to mount guard at *ten,* I was ready
at *nine* : never did any man, or any thing, wait one
moment for me.   Being, at an age *under twenty years,*
raised from Corporal to Serjeant Major *at once,* over the
heads of thirty serjeants, I naturally should have been an
object of envy and hatred ; but this habit of early rising 10
and of rigid adherence to the precepts which I have given
you really subdued these passions : because every one
felt that what I did he had never done, and never could do.
Before my promotion, a clerk was wanted to make out the
morning report of the regiment.   I rendered the clerk
unnecessary ; and, long before any other man was dressed
for the parade, my work for the morning was all done, and
I myself was on the parade, walking, in fine weather, for
an hour perhaps.   My custom was this : to get up in
summer at day-light, and in winter at four o'clock ; shave, 20
dress, even to the putting of my sword-belt over my
shoulder, and having my sword lying on the table before
me, ready to hang by my side.   Then I ate a bit of cheese,
or pork, and bread.   Then I prepared my report, which
was filled up as fast as the companies brought me in the
materials.   After this I had an hour or two to read, before
the time came for any duty out of doors, unless when the
regiment or part of it went out to exercise in the morning.
When this was the case, and the matter was left to me,
I always had it on the ground in such time as that the 30
bayonets glistened in the *rising sun,* a sight which gave
me delight, of which I often think, but which I should in
vain endeavour to describe.   If the *officers* were to go out,
eight or ten o'clock was the hour, sweating the men in the
heat of the day, breaking in upon the time for cooking

their dinner, putting all things out of order and all men out of humour. When I was commander, the men had a long day of leisure before them : they could ramble into the town or into the woods ; go to get raspberries, to catch birds, to catch fish, or to pursue any other recreation, and such of them as chose, and were qualified, to work at their trades. So that here, arising solely from the early habits of one very young man, were pleasant and happy days given to hundreds. . . .

10   I learned grammar when I was a private soldier on the pay of sixpence a day. The edge of my berth, or that of the guard-bed, was my seat to study in ; my knapsack was my book-case ; a bit of board, lying on my lap, was my writing-table ; and the task did not demand any thing like a year of my life. I had no money to purchase candle or oil ; in winter-time it was rarely that I could get any evening-light but that of *the fire*, and only my *turn* even of that. And if I, under such circumstances, and without parent or friend to advise or encourage me, accomplished

20 this undertaking, what excuse can there be for *any youth*, however poor, however pressed with business, or however circumstanced as to room or other conveniences ? To buy a pen or a sheet of paper I was compelled to forego some portion of food, though in a state of half-starvation ; I had no moment of time that I could call my own ; and I had to read and to write amidst the talking, laughing, singing, whistling and brawling of at least half a score of the most thoughtless of men, and that too in the hours of their free- dom from all control. Think not lightly of the *farthing*

30 that I had to give, now and then, for ink, pen, or paper ! That farthing was, alas ! a *great sum* to me ! I was as tall as I am now ; I had great health and great exercise. The whole of the money not expended for us at market was *two-pence a week* for each man. I remember, and well I may ! that upon one occasion I, after all absolutely

necessary expenses, had, on a Friday, made shift to have a half-penny in reserve, which I had destined for the purchase of a *red-herring* in the morning ; but, when I pulled off my clothes at night, so hungry then as to be hardly able to endure life, I found that I had *lost my half-penny !* I buried my head under the miserable sheet and rug, and cried like a child ! : . .

If I have bestowed a large portion of my space on this topic [i. e. grammar], it has been because I know, from experience as well as from observation, that it is of more importance than all the other branches of book-learning put together. It gives you, when you possess it thoroughly, a real and practical superiority over the far greater part of men. How often did I experience this even long before I became what is called an author ! The *Adjutant,* under whom it was my duty to act when I was a Serjeant Major, was, as almost all military officers are, or at least *were,* a very illiterate man, and perceiving that every sentence of mine was in the same form and manner as sentences in *print,* became shy of letting me see pieces of *his* writing. The writing of *orders,* and other things, therefore, fell to me ; and thus, though no nominal addition was made to my pay, and no nominal addition to my authority, I acquired the latter as effectually as if a law had been passed to confer it upon me.

Courtship

(From the *Advice to Young Men.*)

WHEN I first saw my wife, she was *thirteen years old,* and I was within about a month of *twenty-one.* She was the daughter of a Serjeant of artillery, and I was the Serjeant Major of a regiment of foot, both stationed in forts near the city of St. John, in the Province of New Brunswick. I sat in the same room with her, for about an hour, in company with others, and I made up my mind that she

was the very girl for me. That I thought her beautiful is
certain, for that I had always said should be an indispensable
qualification ; but I saw in her what I deemed marks of
that sobriety of *conduct* of which I have said so much, and
which has been by far the greatest blessing of my life.
It was now dead of winter, and, of course, the snow several
feet deep on the ground, and the weather piercing cold.
It was my habit, when I had done my morning's writing,
to go out at break of day to take a walk on a hill at the
foot of which our barracks lay. In about three mornings
after I had first seen her, I had, by an invitation to breakfast with me, got up two young men to join me in my walk ;
and our road lay by the house of her father and mother.
It was hardly light, but she was out on the snow, scrubbing
out a washing-tub. ' That's the girl for me,' said I, when
we had got out of her hearing. One of these young men
came to England soon afterwards ; and he, who keeps an
inn in Yorkshire, came over to Preston, at the time of the
election, to verify whether I were the same man. When
he found that I was, he appeared surprised ; but what was
his surprise when I told him that those tall young men,
whom he saw around me, were the *sons* of that pretty
little girl that he and I saw scrubbing out the washing-tub
on the snow in New Brunswick at day-break in the morning !

From the day that I first spoke to her, I never had
a thought of her ever being the wife of any other man,
more than I had a thought of her being transformed into
a chest of drawers ; and I formed my resolution at once,
to marry her as soon as we could get permission, and to
get out of the army as soon as I could. So that this
matter was, at once, settled as firmly as if written in the
book of fate. At the end of about six months, my regiment,
and I along with it, were removed to FREDERICKTON,
a distance of a *hundred miles*, up the river of ST. JOHN ;
and, which was worse, the artillery were expected to go

off to England a year or two before our regiment ! The
artillery went, and she along with them ; and now it was
that I acted a part becoming a real and sensible lover.
I was aware, that, when she got to that gay place WOOLWICH,
the house of her father and mother, necessarily visited by
numerous persons not the most select, might become un-
pleasant to her, and I did not like, besides, that she should
continue to *work hard*. I had saved a *hundred and fifty
guineas*, the earnings of my early hours, in writing for the
paymaster, the quartermaster, and others, in addition to 10
the savings of my own pay. *I sent her all my money* before
she sailed ; and wrote to her to beg of her, if she found her
home uncomfortable, to hire a lodging with respectable
people : and, at any rate, not to spare the money by any
means, but to buy herself good clothes, and to live without
hard work, until I arrived in England ; and I, in order to
induce her to lay out the money, told her that I should get
plenty more before I came home.

As the malignity of the devil would have it, we were
kept abroad *two years longer* than our time, Mr. PITT 20
(England not being so tame then as she is now) having
knocked up a dust with Spain about Nootka Sound. Oh,
how I cursed Nootka Sound, and poor bawling Pitt too,
I am afraid ! At the end of *four years*, however, home
I came ; landed at Portsmouth, and got my discharge
from the army by the great kindness of poor LORD EDWARD
FITZGERALD, who was then the Major of my regiment.
I found my little girl *a servant of all work* (and hard work it
was), at *five pounds a year*, in the house of a CAPTAIN BRISAC ;
and, without hardly saying a word about the matter, she 30
put into my hands *the whole of my hundred and fifty guineas
unbroken !*

Need I tell the reader what my feelings were ? Need
I tell kind-hearted English parents what effect this anecdote
must have produced on the minds of our children ? Need

I attempt to describe what effect this example ought to
have on every young woman who shall do me the honour
to read this book ?   Admiration of her conduct, and self-
gratulation on this indubitable proof of the soundness of
my own judgment were now added to my love of her
beautiful person.

Now, I do not say that there are not many young women
of this country who would, under similar circumstances,
have acted as my wife did in this case ; on the contrary,
10 I hope, and do sincerely believe, that there are.   But when
her age is considered ; when we reflect that she was living
in a place crowded, literally *crowded*, with gaily dressed and
handsome young men, many of whom really far richer and
in higher rank than I was, and scores of them ready to
offer her their hand ; when we reflect that she was living
amongst young women who put upon their backs every
shilling that they could come at ; when we see her keeping
the bag of gold untouched, and working hard to provide
herself with but mere necessary apparel, and doing this
20 while she was passing from *fourteen to eighteen years of age ;*
when we view the whole of the circumstances, we must say
that here is an example, which, while it reflects honour on
her sex, ought to have weight with every young woman
whose eyes or ears this relation shall reach.

An Idyll of New Brunswick

(From the *Advice to Young Men.*)

THE Province of New Brunswick, in North America, in
which I passed my years from the age of eighteen to that
of twenty-six, consists, in general, of heaps of rocks, in the
interstices of which grow the pine, the spruce, and various
sorts of fir trees, or, where the woods have been burnt
30 down, the bushes of the raspberry or those of the huckle-
berry.   The province is cut asunder lengthwise, by a great

river, called the St. John, about two hundred miles in length and, at half way from the mouth, full a mile wide. Into this main river run innumerable smaller rivers, there called CREEKS. On the sides of these creeks the land is, in places, clear of rocks ; it is, in these places, generally good and productive ; the trees that grow here are the birch, the maple, and others of the deciduous class ; natural meadows here and there present themselves ; and some of these spots far surpass in rural beauty any other that my eyes ever beheld ; the creeks, abounding towards their sources in water-falls of endless variety, as well in form as in magnitude, and always teeming with fish, while water-fowl enliven their surface, and while wild-pigeons of the gayest plumage flutter in thousands upon thousands amongst the branches of the beautiful trees, which sometimes for miles together form an arch over the creeks.

I, in one of my rambles in the woods, in which I took great delight, came to a spot at a very short distance from the source of one of these creeks. Here was every thing to delight the eye, and especially of one like me, who seem to have been born to love rural life and trees and plants of all sorts. Here were about two hundred acres of natural meadow, interspersed with patches of maple trees in various forms and of various extent ; the creek (there about thirty miles from its point of joining the St. John) ran down the middle of the spot, which formed a sort of dish, the high and rocky hills rising all round it, except at the outlet of the creek, and these hills crowned with lofty pines : in the hills were the sources of the creek, the waters of which came down in cascades, for any one of which many a noble-man in England would, if he could transfer it, give a good slice of his fertile estate ; and in the creek, at the foot of the cascades, there were, in the season, salmon the finest in the world, and so abundant, and so easily taken, as to be used for manuring the land.

If nature, in her very best humour, had made a spot for
the express purpose of captivating me, she could not have
exceeded the efforts which she had here made. But I
found something here besides these rude works of nature ;
I found something in the fashioning of which *man* had had
something to do. I found a large and well-built log dwelling
house, standing (in the month of September) on the edge
of a very good field of Indian Corn, by the side of which
there was a piece of buck-wheat just then mowed. I found
10 a homestead, and some very pretty cows. I found all the
things by which an easy and happy farmer is surrounded :
and I found still something besides all these ; something
that was destined to give me a great deal of pleasure and
also a great deal of pain, both in their extreme degree ;
and both of which, in spite of the lapse of forty years, now
make an attempt to rush back into my heart.

Partly from misinformation, and partly from miscalcula-
tion, I had lost my way ; and quite alone, but armed with
my sword and a brace of pistols, to defend myself against
20 the bears, I arrived at the log-house in the middle of
a moonlight night, the hoar frost covering the trees and
the grass. A stout and clamorous dog, kept off by the
gleaming of my sword, waked the master of the house,
who got up, received me with great hospitality, got me
something to eat, and put me into a feather-bed, a thing
that I had been a stranger to for some years. I, being
very tired, had tried to pass the night in the woods,
between the trunks of two large trees, which had fallen
side by side, and within a yard of each other. I had made
30 a nest for myself of dry fern, and had made a covering by
laying boughs of spruce across the trunks of the trees.
But unable to sleep on account of the cold ; becoming
sick from the great quantity of water that I had drunk
during the heat of the day, and being, moreover, alarmed
at the noise of the bears, and lest one of them should find

me in a defenceless state, I had roused myself up, and had
crept along as well as I could. So that no hero of eastern
romance ever experienced a more enchanting change.

I had got into the house of one of those YANKEE
LOYALISTS who, at the close of the revolutionary war
(which, until it had succeeded, was called a rebellion), had
accepted of grants of land in the King's Province of New
Brunswick; and who, to the great honour of England,
had been furnished with all the means of making new and
comfortable settlements. I was suffered to sleep till break- 10
fast time, when I found a table, the like of which I have
since seen so many in the United States, loaded with good
things. The master and the mistress of the house, aged
about fifty, were like what an English farmer and his wife
were half a century ago. There were two sons, tall and
stout, who appeared to have come in from work, and the
youngest of whom was about my age, then twenty-three.
But there was *another member* of the family, aged nineteen,
who (dressed according to the neat and simple fashion of
New England, whence she had come with her parents five 20
or six years before) had her long light-brown hair twisted
nicely up, and fastened on the top of her head, in which
head were a pair of lively blue eyes, associated with features
of which that softness and that sweetness, so characteristic
of American girls, were the predominant expressions, the
whole being set off by a complexion indicative of glowing
health, and forming, figure, movements, and all taken
together, an assemblage of beauties far surpassing any
that I had ever seen but *once* in my life. That *once* was,
too, *two years agone;* and, in such a case and at such an 30
age, two years, two whole years, is a long, long while! It
was a space as long as the eleventh part of my then life!
Here was the *present* against the *absent:* here was the
power of the *eyes* pitted against that of the *memory:* here
were all the senses up in arms to subdue the influence of

the thoughts : here was vanity, here was passion, here
was the spot of all spots in the world, and here were also
the life, and the manners and the habits and the pursuits
that I delighted in : here was every thing that imagination
can conceive, united in a conspiracy against the poor little
brunette in England ! What, then, did I fall in love at
once with this bouquet of lilies and roses ? Oh ! by no
means. I was, however, so enchanted with *the place ;*
I so much enjoyed its tranquillity, the shade of the maple
trees, the business of the farm, the sports of the water and
of the woods, that I stayed at it to the last possible minute,
promising, at my departure, to come again as often as
I possibly could ; a promise which I most punctually
fulfilled.

Winter is the great season for jaunting and *dancing*
(called *frolicking*) in America. In this Province the river
and the creeks were the only *roads* from settlement to
settlement. In summer we travelled in *canoes ;* in winter
in *sleighs* on the ice or snow. During more than two years
I spent all the time I could with my Yankee friends : they
were all fond of me : I talked to them about country affairs,
my evident delight in which they took as a compliment to
themselves : the father and mother treated me as one of
their children ; the sons as a brother ; and the daughter,
who was as modest and as full of sensibility as she was
beautiful, in a way to which a chap much less sanguine
than I was would have given the tenderest interpretation ;
which treatment I, especially in the last-mentioned case,
most cordially repaid.

It is when you meet in company with others of your own
age that you are, in love matters, put most frequently to
the test, and exposed to detection. The next door neighbour
might, in that country, be ten miles off. We used to have
a frolic, sometimes at one house and sometimes at another.
Here, where female eyes are very much on the alert, no

secret can long be kept ; and very soon father, mother, brothers and the whole neighbourhood looked upon the thing as certain, not excepting herself, to whom I, however, had never once even talked of marriage, and had never even told her that I *loved* her. But I had a thousand times done these by *implication*, taking into view the interpretation that she would naturally put upon my looks, appellations, and acts ; and it was of this that I had to accuse myself. Yet I was not a *deceiver ;* for my affection for her was very great : I spent no really pleasant hours but with her : I was uneasy if she showed the slightest regard for any other young man : I was unhappy if the smallest matter affected her health or spirits : I quitted her in dejection, and returned to her with eager delight : many a time, when I could get leave but for a day, I paddled in a canoe two whole succeeding nights, in order to pass that day with her. If this was not love, it was first cousin to it ; for as to any *criminal* intention I no more thought of it, in her case, than if she had been my sister. Many times I put to myself the questions : ' What am I at ? Is not this wrong ? *Why do I go ?* ' But still I went.

Then, further in my excuse, my *prior engagement*, though carefully left unalluded to by both parties, was, in that thin population, and owing to the singular circumstances of it, and to the great talk that there always was about me, *perfectly well known* to her and all her family. It was matter of so much notoriety and conversation in the Province, that GENERAL CARLETON (brother of the late Lord Dorchester), who was the Governor when I was there, when he, about fifteen years afterwards, did me the honour, on his return to England, to come and see me at my house in Duke Street, Westminster, asked, before he went away, to see my *wife*, of whom *he had heard so much* before her marriage. So that here was no *deception* on my part : but

still I ought not to have suffered even the most distant
hope to be entertained by a person so innocent, so amiable,
for whom I had so much affection, and to whose heart
I had no right to give a single twinge. I ought, from the
very first, to have prevented the possibility of her ever
feeling pain on my account. I was young, to be sure ;
but I was old enough to know what was my duty in this
case, and I ought, dismissing my own feelings, to have had
the resolution to perform it.

10   The *last parting* came ; and now came my just punishment ! The time was known to every body, and was
irrevocably fixed ; for I had to move with a regiment, and
the embarkation of a regiment is an *epoch* in a thinly
settled province. To describe this parting would be too
painful even at this distant day, and with this frost of age
upon my head. The kind and virtuous father came forty
miles to see me, just as I was going on board in the river.
His looks and words I have never forgotten. As the vessel
descended, she passed the mouth of *that creek* which I had
20 so often entered with delight ; and though England, and
all that England contained, were before me, I lost sight
of this creek with an aching heart.

On what trifles turn the great events in the life of man !
If I had received a *cool* letter from my intended wife ; if
I had only heard a rumour of any thing from which fickleness in her might have been inferred ; if I had found in her
any, even the smallest, abatement of affection ; if she had
but let go any one of the hundred strings by which she held
my heart : if any of these, never would the world have
30 heard of me. Young as I was ; able as I was as a soldier ;
proud as I was of the admiration and commendations of
which I was the object ; fond as I was, too, of the command
which, at so early an age, my rare conduct and great natural
talents had given me ; sanguine as was my mind, and
brilliant as were my prospects : yet I had seen so much of

the meannesses, the unjust partialities, the insolent pom-
posity, the disgusting dissipations of that way of life, that
I was weary of it : I longed, exchanging my fine laced coat
for the Yankee farmer's home-spun, to be where I should
never behold the supple crouch of servility, and never hear
the hectoring voice of authority, again ; and, on the lonely
banks of this branch-covered creek, which contained (she
out of the question) every thing congenial to my taste and
dear to my heart, I, unapplauded, unfeared, unenvied and
uncalumniated, should have lived and died.   10

First Residence in America : Domestic Happiness

(From the *Advice to Young Men*.)

I BEGAN my young marriage days in and near Philadelphia.
At one of those times to which I have just alluded, in the
middle of the burning hot month of July, I was greatly
afraid of fatal consequences to my wife for want of sleep,
she not having, after the great danger was over, had any
sleep for more than forty-eight hours. All great cities, in
hot countries, are, I believe, full of dogs ; and they, in the
very hot weather, keep up, during the night, a horrible
barking and fighting and howling. Upon the particular
occasion to which I am adverting, they made a noise so 20
terrible and so unremitted that it was next to impossible
that even a person in full health and free from pain should
obtain a minute's sleep. I was, about nine in the evening,
sitting by the bed : ' I do think,' said she, ' that I could go
to sleep *now*, if it were not *for the dogs*.' Down stairs
I went, and out I sallied, in my shirt and trowsers, and
without shoes and stockings ; and, going to a heap of
stones lying beside the road, set to work upon the dogs,
going backward and forward, and keeping them at two
or three hundred yards' distance from the house. I walked 30
thus the whole night, barefooted, lest the noise of my shoes

might possibly reach her ears ; and I remember that the bricks of the causeway were, even in the night, so hot as to be disagreeable to my feet. My exertions produced the desired effect : a sleep of several hours was the consequence ; and at eight o'clock in the morning off went I to a day's business, which was to end at six in the evening.

Women are all patriots of the soil ; and when her neighbours used to ask my wife whether *all* English husbands were like hers, she boldly answered in the 10 affirmative. I had business to occupy the whole of my time, Sundays and week-days, except sleeping hours ; but I used to make time to assist her in the taking care of her baby, and in all sorts of things : get up, light her fire, boil her tea-kettle, carry her up warm water in cold weather, take the child while she dressed herself and got the breakfast ready, then breakfast, get her in water and wood for the day, then dress myself neatly, and sally forth to my business. The moment that was over I used to hasten back to her again ; and I no more thought of spending 20 a moment *away from her*, unless business compelled me, than I thought of quitting the country and going to sea. The *thunder* and *lightning* are tremendous in America, compared with what they are in England. My wife was, at one time, very much afraid of thunder and lightning ; and as is the feeling of all such women, and, indeed, all men too, she wanted company, and particularly her husband, in those times of danger. I knew well, of course, that my presence would not diminish the danger ; but, be I at what I might, if within reach of home, I used to quit my business and 30 hasten to her, the moment I perceived a thunder storm approaching. Scores of miles have I, first and last, *run* on this errand, in the streets of Philadelphia ! The Frenchmen, who were my scholars, used to laugh at me exceedingly on this account ; and sometimes, when I was making an appointment with them, they would say, with a smile and a bow, ' *Sauve la tonnerre toujours, Monsieur Cobbett.*' . . .

For about two or three years after I was married
I, retaining some of my military manners, used, both in
France and America, to *romp* most famously with the girls
that came in my way; till one day, at Philadelphia, my
wife said to me, in a very gentle manner, ' Don't do that :
I do not like it.' That was quite enough : I had never
thought on the subject before : one hair of her head was
more dear to me than all the other women in the world, 10
and this I knew that she knew; but I now saw that this
was not all that she had a right to from me; I saw that
she had the further claim upon me that I should abstain
from every thing that might induce others to believe that
there was any other woman for whom, even if I were at
liberty, I had any affection. I beseech young married
men to bear this in mind; for on some trifle of this
sort the happiness or misery of a long life frequently
turns.

Till I had a second child, no servant ever entered my 20
house, though well able to keep one; and never, in my
whole life, did I live in a house so clean, in such trim order,
and never have I eaten or drunk, or slept or dressed, in
a manner so perfectly to my fancy as I did then. I had
a great deal of business to attend to, that took me a great
part of the day from home; but, whenever I could spare
a minute from business, the child was in my arms; I
rendered the mother's labour as light as I could; any bit
of food satisfied me; when watching was necessary, we
shared it between us; and that famous GRAMMAR for 30
teaching French people English, which has been for thirty
years, and still is, the great work of this kind, throughout
all America, and in every nation in Europe, was written
by me in hours not employed in business, and, in great
part, during my share of the night-watchings over a sick

and then only child, who, after lingering many months, died in my arms. . . .

Love came and rescued me from this state of horrible slavery [the military life]; placed the whole of my time at my own disposal ; made me as free as air ; removed every restraint upon the operations of my mind, naturally disposed to communicate its thoughts to others ; and gave me, for my leisure hours, a companion, who, though deprived of all opportunity of acquiring what is *called*
10 *learning*, had so much good sense, so much useful knowledge, was so innocent, so just in all her ways, so pure in thought, word and deed, so disinterested, so generous, so devoted to me and her children, so free from all disguise, and, withal, so beautiful and so talkative, and in a voice so sweet, so cheering, that I must, seeing the health and the capacity which it had pleased God to give me, have been a *criminal*, if I had done much less than that which I have done ; and I have always said that, if my country feel any gratitude for my labours, that gratitude is due to her full as much
20 as to me.

Return to England, 1800

(From *A Year's Residence in the United States*, 1818–19.)

WHEN I returned to England, in 1800, after an absence from the country parts of it of sixteen years, the trees, the hedges, even the parks and woods, seemed so *small !* It made me laugh to hear little gutters, that I could jump over, called *Rivers !* The Thames was but a ' *Creek !* ' But when, in about a month after my arrival in London, I went to *Farnham*, the place of my birth, what was my surprise ! Every thing was become so pitifully *small !* I had to cross, in my post-chaise, the long and dreary
30 heath of Bagshot. Then, at the end of it, to mount a hill, called Hungry Hill ; and from that hill I knew that I should

look down into the beautiful and fertile valley of Farnham. My heart fluttered with impatience, mixed with a sort of fear, to see all the scenes of my childhood ; for I had learnt before the death of my father and mother. There is a hill, not far from the town, called *Crooksbury Hill*, which rises up out of a flat, in the form of a *cone*, and is planted with Scotch fir trees. Here I used to take the eggs and young ones of crows and magpies. This hill was a famous object in the neighbourhood. It served as the superlative degree of height. ' *As high as Crooksbury Hill*' meant, with us, the utmost degree of height. Therefore, the first object that my eyes sought was this hill. *I could not believe my eyes !* Literally speaking, I for a moment thought the famous hill removed, and a little heap put in its stead ; for I had seen in New Brunswick a single rock, or hill of solid rock, ten times as big, and four or five times as high ! The post-boy, going down hill, and not a bad road, whisked me, in a few minutes to the Bush Inn, from the garden of which I could see the prodigious *sand hill*, where I had begun my gardening works. What a *nothing !* But now came rushing into my mind, all at once, my pretty little garden, my little blue smock-frock, my little nailed shoes, my pretty pigeons that I used to feed out of my hands, the last kind words and tears of my gentle and tender-hearted and affectionate mother ! I hastened back into the room. If I had looked a moment longer, I should have dropped. When I came to reflect, *what a change !* I looked down at my dress. What a change ! What scenes I had gone through ! How altered my state ! I had dined the day before at a secretary of state's in company with Mr. *Pitt*, and had been waited upon by men in gaudy liveries ! I had had nobody to assist me in the world. No teachers of any sort. Nobody to shelter me from the consequence of bad, and no one to counsel me to good, behaviour. I felt proud. The distinctions of rank, birth, and wealth, all became nothing in my eyes ; and from that moment (less than a month after my arrival in England) I resolved never to bend before them.

Life at Fairthorn, Botley

(From the *Advice to Young Men*.)

THE first thing of all [in the education of his children] was *health*, which was secured by the deeply-interesting and never-ending *sports of the field* and *pleasures of the garden*. Luckily these things were treated of in *books* and *pictures* of endless variety ; so that on *wet days*, in *long evenings*, these came into play. A large, strong table, in
10 the middle of the room, their mother sitting at her work, used to be surrounded with them, the baby, if big enough, set up in a high chair. Here were inkstands, pens, pencils, India rubber, and paper, all in abundance, and every one scrabbled about as he or she pleased. There were prints of animals of all sorts ; books treating of them : others treating of gardening, of flowers, of husbandry, of hunting, coursing, shooting, fishing, planting, and, in short, of every thing with regard to which *we had something to do*. One would be trying to imitate a bit of my writing, another
20 *drawing* the pictures of some of our dogs or horses, a third poking over *Bewick's Quadrupeds* and picking out what he said about them ; but our book of never-failing resource was the *French* MAISON RUSTIQUE, or FARM-HOUSE, which, it is said, was the book that first tempted DUQUESNOIS (I think that was the name), the famous physician, in the reign of Louis XIV., *to learn to read*. Here are all the *four-legged animals*, from the horse down to the mouse, *portraits* and all ; all the *birds, reptiles, insects ;* all the modes of rearing, managing, and using the tame ones ; all
30 the modes of taking the wild ones, and of destroying those that are mischievous ; all the various traps, springs, nets ;

all the implements of husbandry and gardening ; all the
labours of the field and the garden exhibited, as well as the
rest, in plates ; and, there was I, in my leisure moments,
to join this inquisitive group, to read the *French*, and tell
them what it meaned in *English*, when the picture did not
sufficiently explain itself. I never have been without a copy
of this book for forty years, except during the time that
I was fleeing from the dungeons of CASTLEREAGH and
SIDMOUTH, in 1817 ; and, when I got to Long Island, the
first book I bought was another MAISON RUSTIQUE. . . .   10

What need had we of *schools ?* What need of *teachers ?*
What need of *scolding* and *force*, to induce children to read,
write, and love books ? What need of *cards, dice*, or of any
games to ' *kill time*,' but, in fact, to implant in the infant
heart a love of *gaming*, one of the most destructive of all
human vices ? We did not want to ' *kill time* : ' we were
always *busy*, wet weather or dry weather, winter or summer.
There was no *force* in any case ; no *command* ; no *authority* ;
none of these was ever wanted. To teach the children the
habit of *early rising* was a great object ; and every one 20
knows how young people cling to their beds, and how loth
they are to go to those beds. This was a capital matter ;
because here were *industry* and *health* both at stake. Yet,
I avoided *command* even here ; and merely offered a *reward*.
The child that was *down stairs* first, was called the LARK
for that day ; and, further, *sat at my right hand at dinner*.
They soon discovered, that, to rise early, they must *go to
bed early* ; and thus was this most important object secured,
with regard to girls as well as boys. Nothing more incon-
venient, and, indeed, more disgusting, than to have to do 30
with girls, or young women, who lounge in bed. . . .

This is the age, too, to teach children to be *trust-worthy*,
and to be *merciful* and *humane*. We lived *in a garden* of
about two acres, partly kitchen-garden with walls, partly
shrubbery and trees, and partly grass. There were the

peaches, as tempting as any that ever grew, and yet as safe
from fingers as if no child were ever in the garden. It was
not necessary to *forbid*. The blackbirds, the thrushes, the
whitethroats, and even that very shy bird the goldfinch,
had their nests and bred up their young-ones in great
abundance all about this little spot, constantly the play-
place of six children ; and one of the latter had its nest,
and brought up its young-ones, in a *raspberry-bush*, within
two yards of a walk, and at the time that we were gathering
10 the ripe raspberries. We give *dogs*, and justly, great credit
for sagacity and memory ; but the following two most
curious instances, which I should not venture to state, if
there were not so many witnesses to the facts, in my
neighbours at Botley, as well as in my own family, will
show that *birds* are not, in this respect, inferior to the
canine race. All country people know that the *skylark* is
a very shy bird ; that its abode is the open fields : that it
settles on the ground only ; that it seeks safety in the
wideness of space ; that it avoids enclosures, and is never
20 seen in gardens. A part of our ground was a grass-plat of
about *forty rods*, or a quarter of an acre, which, one year,
was left to be mowed for hay. A pair of larks, coming out
of the fields into the middle of a pretty populous village,
chose to make their nest in the middle of this little spot, and
at not more than about *thirty-five yards* from one of the doors
of the house, in which there were about twelve persons
living, and six of those children, who had constant access
to all parts of the ground. There we saw the cock rising
up and singing, then taking his turn upon the eggs ; and
30 by-and-by, we observed him cease to sing, and saw them
both *constantly engaged in bringing food to the young ones*.
No unintelligible hint to fathers and mothers of the human
race, who have, before marriage, taken delight in *music*.
But the time came for *mowing the grass !* I waited a good
many days for the brood to get away ; but, at last,

I determined on the day ; and if the larks were there still, to leave a patch of grass standing round them. In order not to keep them in dread longer than necessary, I brought three able mowers, who would cut the whole in about an hour; and as the plat was nearly circular, set them to mow *round*, beginning at the outside. And now for sagacity indeed ! The moment the men began to whet their scythes, the two old larks began to flutter over the nest, and to make a great clamour. When the men began to mow, they flew round and round, stooping so low, when near 10 the men, as almost to touch their bodies, making a great chattering at the same time ; but before the men had got round with the second swarth, they flew to the nest, and away they went, young ones and all, across the river, at the foot of the ground, and settled in the long grass in my neighbour's orchard.

The other instance relates to a HOUSE-MARTEN. It is well known that these birds build their nests under the eaves of inhabited houses, and sometimes under those of door porches ; but we had one that built its nest *in the* 20 *house,* and upon the top of a common doorcase, the door of which opened into a room out of the main passage into the house. Perceiving the marten had begun to build its nest here, we kept the front-door open in the daytime ; but were obliged to fasten it at night. It went on, had eggs, young ones, and the young ones flew. I used to open the door in the morning early, and then the birds carried on their affairs till night. The next *year* the MARTEN came again, and had *another brood in the same place.* It found its *old nest;* and having repaired it, and put it in order, 30 went on again in the former way ; and it would, I dare say, have continued to come to the end of its life, if we had remained there so long, notwithstanding there were six healthy children in the house, making just as much noise as they pleased.

In Prison, July 1810–*July* 1812

(From the *Advice to Young Men.*)

In this happy state we lived, until the year 1810, when the government laid its merciless fangs upon me, dragged me from these delights, and *crammed me into a jail amongst felons ;* of which I shall have to speak more fully when, in the last Number, I come to speak of the duties of THE CITIZEN. This added to the difficulties of my task of *teaching ;* for now I was snatched away from the *only* scene in which it could, as I thought, properly be executed. But even these difficulties were got over. The blow was,
10 to be sure, a terrible one ; and, oh God ! how was it felt by these poor children ! It was in the month of July when the horrible sentence was passed upon me. My wife, having left her children in the care of her good and affectionate sister, was in London, waiting to know the doom of her husband. When the news arrived at Botley, the three boys, one eleven, another nine, and the other seven, years old, were hoeing cabbages in that garden which had been the source of so much delight. When the account of the savage sentence was brought to them, the youngest could not, for
20 some time, be made to understand what a *jail* was ; and, when he did, he, all in a tremor, exclaimed, ' Now I'm sure, William, that PAPA is not in a place *like that !* ' The other, in order to disguise his tears and smother his sobs, fell to work with the hoe, and *chopped about like a blind person.* This account, when it reached me, affected me more, filled me with deeper resentment, than any other circumstance. And, oh ! how I despise the wretches who talk of my *vindictiveness ;* of my *exultation* at the confusion of those who inflicted those sufferings ! How I despise the base
30 creatures, the crawling slaves, the callous and cowardly hypocrites, who affect to be ' *shocked* ' (tender souls !) at my expressions of *joy*, and at the death of Gibbs, Ellen-

borough, Perceval, Liverpool, Canning, and the rest of the
tribe that I have already seen out, and at the fatal workings
of *that system*, for endeavouring to check which I was thus
punished ! How I despise these wretches, and how I, above
all things, enjoy their ruin, and anticipate their utter
beggary ! What ! I am to forgive, am I, injuries like this ;
and that, too, without any *atonement ?* Oh, no ! I have
not so read the Holy Scriptures ; I have not, from them,
learned that I am not to rejoice at the fall of unjust foes ;
and it makes a part of my happiness to be able *to tell* 10
millions of men that I do thus rejoice, and that I have
the means of calling on so many just and merciful men to
rejoice along with me.

Now, then, the *book-learning* was *forced* upon us. I had
a *farm* in hand. It was necessary that I should be constantly informed of what was doing. I gave *all the orders,*
whether as to purchases, sales, ploughing, sowing, breeding ;
in short, with regard to every thing, and the things were
endless in number and variety, and always full of interest.
My eldest son and daughter could now write well and fast. 20
One or the other of these was always at Botley ; and I had
with me (having hired the best part of the keeper's house)
one or two, besides either this brother or sister ; the mother
coming up to town about once in two or three months,
leaving the house and children in the care of her sister.
We had a HAMPER, with a lock and two keys, which came
up once a week, or oftener, bringing me fruit and all sorts
of country fare, for the carriage of which, cost free, I was
indebted to as good a man as ever God created, the late
Mr. GEORGE ROGERS, of Southampton, who, in the prime 30
of life, died deeply lamented by thousands, but by none
more deeply than by me and my family, who have to thank
him, and the whole of his excellent family, for benefits and
marks of kindness without number.

This HAMPER, which was always, at both ends of the

line, looked for with the most lively feelings, became our
school. It brought me *a journal* of *labours, proceedings,* and
occurrences, written on paper of shape and size uniform,
and so contrived, as to margins, as to admit of binding.
The journal used, when my son was the writer, to be
interspersed with drawings of our dogs, colts, or any thing
that he wanted me to have a correct idea of. The hamper
brought me plants, bulbs, and the like, that I might *see*
the size of them ; and always every one sent his or her
10 *most beautiful flowers ;* the earliest violets, and primroses,
and cowslips, and blue-bells ; the earliest twigs of trees ;
and, in short, every thing that they thought calculated to
delight me. The moment the hamper arrived, I, casting
aside every thing else, set to work to answer *every question,*
to give new directions, and to add anything likely to give
pleasure at Botley. *Every* hamper brought one ' *letter,*'
as they called it, if not more, from every child ; and to
every letter I wrote *an answer,* sealed up and sent to the
party, being sure that that was the way to produce other
20 and better letters ; for, though they could not read what
I wrote, and though their own consisted at first of mere
scratches, and afterwards, for a while, of a few words
written down for them to imitate, I always thanked them
for their ' *pretty letter* ' ; and never expressed any wish to
see them *write better ;* but took care to write in a very
neat and plain hand *myself,* and to do up my letter in
a very neat manner.

Thus, while the ferocious tigers thought I was doomed
to incessant mortification, and to rage that must extinguish
30 my mental powers, I found in my children, and in their
spotless and courageous and most affectionate mother,
delights to which the callous hearts of those tigers were
strangers.

The Election at Coventry, January 1820

(From *The Political Register.*)

THE way I managed the brutes was well calculated to
sting them and their employers to madness. I have,
perhaps, as much of *good-humour* on my countenance,
naturally, and as little of the gloomy, as any man that
ever lived ; and I defy the Rich Ruffians of Coventry to
say that the *thousand pounds a day* (for that was about
the sum) which they expended on their savages ever took
away that good humour for a moment ! My way was to
stand and look upon the yelling beasts with a most good-
humoured smile ; turning my head now and then, leaning 10
it, as it were to take different views of the same person, or
the same group. I now and then substituted something
of *curiosity* instead of the general total *unconcern* that was
seated upon my face. Now and then I would put my
mouth close to the ear of some friend that stood by me,
and then point to some beast that was foaming with rage,
giving him at the same time a laughing look, such as we
bestow upon a dog that is chained up and barking at us.
Then another time, when half a dozen fresh-drenched brutes
were bursting forth close under my nose, I would stretch 20
up my neck, and look, with apparently great curiosity and
anxiousness towards a distant part of the crowd, as if to
ascertain what was passing there ; and this I would do
with so much apparent earnestness and continue in that
attitude so long, that the beasts really seemed, sometimes,
as if they were going mad ! I never had so good an
opportunity to *philosophise* before. A friend, who saw
these man-brutes, said that they shook his faith in *the
immortality of the soul.* But I see no reason at all for any
such conclusion. I believe, and have long believed, that 30
there are more *sorts* of men than there are of dogs. The
mere circumstance of a creature's walking upon *two legs*

is no proof that he is of the same *sort* or *kind* as I am, or as any other man of mind is. . . .

This, or something very much like it, was the train of my ideas, while contemplating the horrid groups at the Booth. A parcel of frogs or toads croaking in a pool of dirty water could as soon have disturbed the muscles of my face as these miserable and degraded things could have done it. When one of these beasts attempted to strike me, however, the feeling became *different!* He reached over the side of
10 the Booth, and caught me by the collar, which was instantly repaid by a blow in his face, for, as Swift says, ' if a *flea* or a *louse* bite me, I'll kill it, if I can.'

At a Hostile Meeting, Lewes, January 9, 1822
(From the *Rural Rides*.)

No sooner had Hitchins done, than up started Mr. Ingram, a farmer of Rottendean, who was the second person in the drama (for all had been duly prepared), and moved that I should be *put out of the room!* Some few of the Webb Hallites, joined by about six or eight of the dark, dirty-faced, half-whiskered, tax-eaters from Brighton (which is only eight miles off) joined in this cry. I rose, that they
20 might see the man that they had to put out. Fortunately *for themselves* not one of them attempted to approach me. They were like the mice that resolved that a bell should be put round the cat's neck!—However, a considerable hubbub took place. At last, however, the chairman, Mr. Kemp, whose conduct was fair and manly, having given my health, I proceeded to address the company.

The Ruling Passion
(From *Rural Rides* : Stanford Park, September 1826.)

THE house and stables and courts are such as they ought to be for the great estate that surrounds them ; and the park is everything that is beautiful. . . .

' Well, then,' says the devil of laziness, ' and could you not be contented to live here all the rest of your life ; and never again pester yourself with the cursed politics ? ' ' Why, I think I have laboured enough. Let others work now. And such a pretty place for coursing and for hare-hunting and woodcock shooting, I dare say ; and then those pretty wild ducks in the water, and the flowers and the grass and the trees, and all the birds in spring, and the fresh air, and never, never again to be stifled with the smoke that from the infernal Wen ascendeth for ever more, 10 and that every easterly wind brings to choke me at Kensington ! ' The *last word* of this soliloquy carried me back, slap, to my own study (very much unlike that which I am in), and bade me think of the GRIDIRON ; bade me think of the complete triumph that I have yet to enjoy : promised me the pleasure of seeing a million of trees of my own, and sown by my own hands this very year. Ah ! but the hares and the pheasants and the wild ducks ! Yes, but the delight of seeing Prosperity Robinson hang his head for shame. . . . Yes, but, then, the flowers and the 20 birds and the sweet air ! What, then, shall Canning . . . never again be told of Six-Acts and of his wish ' to extinguish that *accursed torch of discord for ever !* ' Oh ! God forbid ! farewell hares and dogs and birds ! what, shall Sidmouth, then, never again hear of his *Power of Imprisonment Bill*, of his *Circular*, of his *Letter of Thanks to the Manchester Yeomanry !* I really jumped up when this thought came athwart my mind, and, without thinking of the breakfast, said to George, who was sitting by me, ' Go, George, and tell them to saddle the horses ; ' for it seemed to me that 30 I had been meditating some crime. Upon George asking me whether I would not stop to breakfast ? I bade him not order the horses out yet ; and here we are, waiting for breakfast.

AMERICA

An Incident in Congress, March 1795

(From *Porcupine's Gazette*.)

THE bill had been read, I believe, a second time, and was about to undergo a third reading, when *Giles* (a man famous for low cunning, and for associating in his manners and disposition those tyger and monkey-like qualities so conspicuous in the French) arose, and brought forward a clause to prevent *titled foreigners from being admitted to the invaluable rights of citizens of America, 'till they had explicitly renounced their titles in open court.* This amendment to the bill he accompanied with certain observations
10 respecting the great danger to be apprehended from an influx of foreign noblemen, which the republican successes in Europe, and the high reputation of America would most certainly produce. Giles acted his part, on this occasion, with so much theatrical art, with so much gravity and even alarm in his look and manner, that his friend Madison, who was not previously consulted, really took him to be in earnest, and rendered himself everlastingly ridiculous by the speech which he made in seconding his motion. After saying that he expected, in a short time, to see *the peerage*
20 *of Great Britain come thronging to these States*, and promising that he would condescend to *sympathize* with them, and to receive them with that hospitality and tenderness to which *misfortune* is entitled, he declared, however, that no earthly consideration, no *charity*, no *compassion*, should induce him to suffer the revival of their hereditary pretensions in a country where the people were the only lawful *sovereign*, and where to attempt to enjoy honours and titles derived from any other source would be an act of *treason*, which he,

for one, would endeavour to punish at the *risk of losing the last drop of his blood !*

Never was a more ludicrous farce acted to a bursting audience. Madison is a little bow-legged man, at once stiff and slender. His countenance has that sour aspect, that conceited screw, which pride would willingly mould into an expression of disdain, if it did not find the features too skinny and too scanty for its purpose. His thin sleek hair, and the niceness of his garments are indicative of that economical cleanliness which expostulates with the 10 shoe-boy and the washer-woman, which flees from the dangers of a gutter, and which boasts of wearing a shirt for three days without rumpling the ruffle. In short, he has, take him altogether, precisely the prim, mean, prig-like look of a corporal mechanic, and, were he ushered into your parlour, you would wonder why he came without his measure and his sheers.

Such (and with a soul which would disgrace any other tenement than that which contains it) is the mortal who stood up upon its two legs, confidently predicted the over- 20 throw of the British monarchy, and anticipated the pleasure of feeding its illustrious nobles with his orts !

Farewell to America, June 1800

(From *Porcupine's Gazette.*)

You will, doubtless, be astonished that after having had such a smack of the sweets of *liberty*, I should think of rising thus abruptly from the feast ; but this astonishment will cease when you consider that under a general term things diametrically opposite in their natures are frequently included, and that flavours are not more various than tastes. Thus, for instance, nourishment of every species is called *food*, and we *all* like food ; but while one is partial 30 to roast beef and plumb pudding, another is distractedly fond of flummery and mush ; so is it with respect to *liberty*, of which, out of its infinite variety of sorts, yours unfortunately happens to be precisely that sort which I do not like.

When people care not two straws for each other, ceremony at parting is mere grimace ; and as I have long felt the most perfect indifference with regard to a vast majority of those whom I now address, I shall spare myself the trouble of a ceremonious farewell. Let me not, however, depart from you with indiscriminating contempt. If no man ever had so many and such malignant foes, no one ever had more friends, and those more kind, more sincere, and more faithful. If I have been unjustly vilified by some, others have extolled me far beyond my merits ; if the savages of the city have scared my children in the cradle, those children have, for their father's sake, been soothed and caressed by the affectionate, the gentle, the generous inhabitants of the country, under whose hospitable roofs I have spent some of the happiest hours of my life.

Thus and *thus*, Americans, will I ever speak of you. In a very little time I shall be beyond the reach of your friendship or your malice ; beyond the hearing of your commendations or your curses ; but being out of your power will alter neither my sentiments nor my words. As I have never spoken any thing but truth to you, so I will never speak any thing but truth of you : the heart of a Briton revolts at an emulation in baseness ; and though you have, as a nation, treated me most ungratefully and unjustly, I scorn to repay you with ingratitude and injustice.

To my friends, who are also the real friends of America, I wish that peace and happiness which virtue ought to ensure, but which, I greatly fear, they will not find ; and as to my enemies, I can wish them no severer scourge than that which they are preparing for themselves and their country. With this I depart for my native land, where neither the moth of *Democracy*, nor the rust of *Federalism* doth corrupt, and where thieves do not, with impunity, break through and steal five thousand dollars at a time.

Long Island : Absence of Cottage Gardens

(From *A Year's Residence in the United States*, published 1822.)

THE *dwellings and gardens, and little out-houses* of labourers, which form so striking a feature of beauty in England, and especially in Kent, Sussex, Surrey, and Hampshire, and which constitute a sort of fairy-land, when compared with those of the labourers in France, are what I, for my part, most feel the want of seeing upon Long Island. Instead of the neat and warm little cottage, the yard, cow-stable, pig-sty, hen-house, all in 10 miniature, and the garden nicely laid out, and the paths bordered with flowers, while the cottage door is crowned with a garland of roses or honey-suckle ; instead of these, we here see the labourer content with a shell of boards, while all around him is as barren as the sea-beach ; though the natural earth would send melons, the finest in the world, creeping round his door, and though there is no English shrub, or flower, which will not grow and flourish here. This want of attention in such cases is hereditary from the first settlers. They found land so plenty that 20 they treated small spots with contempt. Besides, the *example* of neatness was wanting. There were no gentlemen's gardens, kept as clean as drawing-rooms, with grass as even as a carpet. From endeavouring to imitate perfection men arrive at mediocrity ; and those who never have seen or heard of perfection, in these matters, will naturally be slovens.

The Homes of America

(From *A Year's Residence in the United States*.)

LANCASTER is a pretty place. No *fine* buildings ; but no *mean* ones. Nothing *splendid* and nothing *beggarly*. The people of this town seem to have had the prayer of HAGAR granted them : ' Give me, O Lord, neither *poverty* nor *riches*.' Here are none of those poor, wretched habitations which sicken the sight at the *outskirts* of cities and towns in England ; those abodes of the poor creatures who have been reduced to beggary by the cruel extortions of the rich and powerful. And this remark applies to *all*
10 the towns of America that I have ever seen. This is a fine part of America. *Big Barns*, and modest dwelling houses. Barns of *stone*, a *hundred feet* long and *forty wide*, with two floors, and raised roads to go into them, so that the waggons go into the *first floor up-stairs*. Below are stables, stalls, pens, and all sorts of conveniences. Up-stairs are rooms for threshed corn and grain ; for tackle, for meal, for all sorts of things. In the front (South) of the barn is the cattle yard. These are very fine buildings. And, then, all about them looks so comfortable, and gives such manifest
20 proofs of ease, plenty, and happiness ! Such is the country of WILLIAM PENN's settling ! It is a curious thing to observe the *farm-houses* in this country. They consist, almost without exception, of a considerably large and a very neat house, with sash windows, and of a *small house*, which seems to have been *tacked on* to the large one ; and, the proportion they bear to each other, in point of dimensions, is, as nearly as possible, the proportion of size between a *Cow* and *her Calf*, the latter a month old. But, as to the *cause*, the process has been the opposite in
30 this instance of the works of nature, for it is *the large house which has grown out of the small one*. The father, or grandfather, while he was toiling for his children, lived in

the small house, constructed chiefly by himself, and consisting of rude materials. The means, accumulated in the
small house, enabled a son to rear the large one ; and
though, when *pride* enters the door, the small house is
sometimes demolished, few sons in America have the folly
or want of feeling to commit such acts of filial ingratitude
and of real self-abasement. For what inheritance so
valuable and so honourable can a son enjoy as the proofs
of his father's industry and virtue ? The progress of
wealth and ease and enjoyment, evinced by this regular 10
increase of the size of the farmers' dwellings, is a spectacle,
at once pleasing, in a very high degree, in itself ; and, in
the same degree, it speaks the praise of the system of
government under which it has taken place. What a contrast with the farm-houses in England ! There the *little*
farm-houses are falling into ruins, or are actually become
cattle-sheds, or, at best, *cottages*, as they are called, to
contain a miserable labourer, who ought to have been
a farmer, as his grandfather was.

American Hospitality

(From *A Year's Residence in the United States*.)

IT is not with a little bit of dry toast, so neatly put in 20
a rack ; a bit of butter so round and small, a little milk
pot so pretty and so empty ; an egg *for you*, the host and
hostess *not liking eggs*. It is not with looks that seem to
say, ' don't eat too much, for the tax gatherer is coming.'
It is not thus that you are received in America. You are
not much *asked*, not much *pressed*, to eat and drink ; but
such an abundance is spread before you, and so hearty and
so cordial is your reception, that you instantly lose all
restraint, and are tempted to feast whether you be hungry
or not. And, though the *manner* and *style* are widely 30
different in different houses, the *abundance* every where

prevails. This is the strength of the government : a happy people : and no government ought to have any other strength.

But you may say, perhaps, that plenty, however great, is not *all* that is wanted. Very true : for the *mind* is of more account than the carcass. But here is mind too. These repasts, amongst people of any figure, come forth under the superintendance of industrious and accomplished house-wifes, or their daughters, who all *read a good deal,* ₁₀ and in whom that gentle treatment from parents and husbands, which arises from an absence of racking anxiety, has created an habitual, and even an hereditary *good humour.* These ladies can converse with you upon almost any subject, and the ease and gracefulness of their behaviour are surpassed by those of none of even our best-tempered English women. They fade at an earlier age than in England ; but, till then, they are as beautiful as the women in *Cornwall,* which contains, to my thinking, the prettiest women in our country. However, young or old, ₂₀ blooming or fading, well or ill, rich or poor, they still preserve their *good humour.*

American Manhood

(From *A Year's Residence in the United States.*)

It is, too, of importance to know *what sort* of labourers these Americans are ; for, though a labourer is a labourer, still there is some difference in them ; and these Americans are *the best that I ever saw.* They mow *four acres* of *oats, wheat, rye,* or *barley* in a day, and, with a cradle, lay it so smooth in the swarths that it is tied up in sheaves with the greatest neatness and ease. They mow *two acres and a half of grass* in a day, and they do the work well. And the ₃₀ crops, upon an average, are all, except the wheat, *as heavy* as in England. The English farmer will want nothing more than these facts to convince him that the labour, after all, is not so *very dear*.

The causes of these performances, so far beyond those in England, is first, the men are *tall* and well built ; they are *bony* rather than fleshy ; and they *live*, as to food, as well as man can live. And, secondly, they have been *educated* to do much in a day. The farmer here generally is at the *head* of his ' boys,' as they, in the kind language of the country, are called. Here is the best of examples. My old and beloved friend, Mr. JAMES PAUL, used, at the age of nearly *sixty* to go at *the head of his mowers*, though his fine farm was his own, and though he might, in other respects, be called a rich man ; and, I have heard, that Mr. ELIAS HICKS, the famous Quaker Preacher, who lives about nine miles from this spot, has this year, at *seventy* years of age, cradled down four acres of rye in a day.

Besides the great quantity of work performed by the American labourer, his *skill*, the *versatility* of his talent, is a great thing. Every man can use an *ax*, a *saw*, and a *hammer*. Scarcely one who cannot do any job at rough carpentering, and mend a plough or a waggon. Very few indeed who cannot kill and dress pigs and sheep, and many of them Oxen and Calves. Every farmer is a *neat* butcher ; a butcher for *market* ; and, of course, ' the boys ' must learn. This is a great convenience. It makes you so independent as to a main part of the means of house-keeping. All are *ploughmen*. In short, a good labourer here can do *any thing* that is to be done upon a farm.

So that our men, who come from England, must not expect that, in these *common labours* of the country, they are to surpass, or even equal, these ' *Yankees*,' who, of all men that I ever saw, are the most *active* and the most *hardy*. They skip over a fence like a greyhound. They will catch you a pig in an open field by *racing* him down ; and they are afraid of nothing. This was the sort of stuff

that filled the *frigates* of DECATUR, HULL, and BRAINBRIDGE.
No wonder that they triumphed when opposed to poor
pressed creatures, worn out by length of service and ill-
usage, and encouraged by no hope of fair-play. My LORD
COCHRANE said, in his place in parliament, that it would
be so ; and so it was. Poor CASHMAN, that brave Irishman,
with his dying breath, accused the government and the
merchants of England of withholding from him his pittance
of prize money ! Ought not such a vile, robbing, murderous
10 system to be destroyed.

Of the same active, hardy, and brave stuff, too, was
composed the army of JACKSON, who drove the invaders
into the Gulph of Mexico, and who would have driven into
the same Gulph the army of Waterloo, and the heroic
gentleman, too, who lent his hand to the murder of Marshal
Ney. This is the stuff that stands between the rascals,
called the Holy Alliance, and the slavery of the whole
civilized world. This is the stuff that gives us Englishmen
an asylum ; that gives us time to breathe ; that enables
20 us to deal our tyrants blows, which, without the existence
of this stuff, they never would receive. This America, this
scene of happiness under a free government, is the beam in
the eye, the thorn in the side, the worm in the vitals, of
every despot upon the face of the earth.

THE FACE OF ENGLAND

The most beautiful places in the Land

(From *Rural Rides*, October 2, 1826.)

ALONG here [i. e. from Swindon to Burghclere] the country is rather *too bare:* here, until you come to Auborne, or Aldbourne, there are *no meadows* in the valleys, and no trees, even round the homesteads. This, therefore, is too naked to please me ; but I love *the downs* so much that, if I had to choose, I would live even here, and especially I would *farm* here, rather than on the banks of the Wye in Herefordshire, in the vale of Gloucester, of Worcester, or of Evesham, or even in what the Kentish men call their ' garden of Eden.' I have now seen (for I have, years back, 10 seen the vales of Taunton, Glastonbury, Honiton, Dorchester and Sherborne) what are deemed the richest and most beautiful parts of England ; and if called upon to name the spot which I deem the brightest and most beautiful and, of its extent, *best* of all, I should say the villages of *North Bovant and Bishopstrow*, between Heytesbury and Warminster in Wiltshire ; for there is, as appertaining to rural objects, *everything* that I delight in. Smooth and verdant downs in hills and valleys of endless variety as to height and depth and shape ; rich corn-land, unencumbered by 20 fences ; meadows in due proportion, and those watered at pleasure ; and, lastly, the homesteads, and villages, sheltered in winter and shaded in summer by lofty and beautiful trees ; to which may be added roads never dirty and a stream never dry.

The Inn at Everley in Wiltshire

(From *Rural Rides*, August 27, 1826.)

THIS inn is one of the nicest, and, in summer, one of the
pleasantest, in England ; for I think that my experience in
this way will justify me in speaking thus positively. The
house is large, the yard and the stables good, the landlord
a farmer also, and, therefore, no cribbing your horses in
hay or straw and yourself in eggs and cream. The garden,
which adjoins the south side of the house, is large, of good
shape, has a terrace on one side, lies on the slope, consists
of well-disposed clumps of shrubs and flowers, and of short
10 grass very neatly kept. In the lower part of the garden
there are high trees, and, amongst these, the tulip-tree and
the live-oak. Beyond the garden is a large clump of lofty
sycamores, and in these a most populous rookery, in which,
of all things in the world, I delight. The village, which
contains 301 souls, lies to the north of the inn, but adjoining
its premises. All the rest, in every direction, is bare down
or open arable. I am now sitting at one of the southern
windows of this inn, looking across the garden towards the
rookery. It is nearly sun-setting ; the rooks are skimming
20 and curving over the tops of the trees ; while under the
branches I see a flock of several hundred sheep coming
nibbling their way in from the down and going to their
fold. . . .

A very fine morning ; a man, *eighty-two years of age*, just
beginning to mow the short-grass in the garden : I thought
it, even when I was young, the *hardest work* that man had
to do. To *look on*, this work seems nothing ; but it tries
every sinew in your frame if you go upright and do your
work well. This old man never knew how to do it well,
30 and he stoops, and he hangs his scythe wrong ; but with
all this, it must be a surprising man to mow short-grass

as well as he does at *eighty*. *I wish I* may be able to mow short-grass at eighty ! That's all I have to say of the matter.

The Wiltshire Downs

(From *Rural Rides*, October 1825.)

OF these 13 miles (from Winchester to Whitchurch) we rode about eight or nine upon the *green-sward*, or over fields equally smooth. And here is one great pleasure of living in countries of this sort : no sloughs, no ditches, no nasty dirty lanes, and the hedges, where there are any, are more for boundary marks than for fences. Fine for hunting and coursing : no impediments ; no gates to open ; 10 nothing to impede the dogs, the horses, or the view. The water is not *seen running ;* but the great bed of chalk *holds it*, and the sun draws it up for the benefit of the grass and the corn ; and whatever inconvenience is experienced from the necessity of deep wells, and of driving sheep and cattle far to water, is amply made up for by the goodness of the water, and by the complete absence of floods, of drains, of ditches and of water-furrows. As *things now are*, however, these countries have one great draw-back : the poor day-labourers suffer from the want of fuel, and 20 they have nothing but their *bare pay.* For these reasons they are greatly worse off than those of the *woodland countries* ; and it is really surprising what a difference there is between the faces that you see here, and the round, red faces that you see in the *wealds* and the *forests*, particu- larly in Sussex, where the labourers *will* have a *meat- pudding* of some sort or other ; and where they *will* have *a fire* to sit by in the winter.

The Valley of the Avon in Wiltshire

(From *Rural Rides*, August 28, 1826.)

THE shepherd showed me the way towards Milton; and at the end of about a mile, from the top of a very high part of the down, with a steep slope towards the valley, I first saw this *Valley of Avon ;* and a most beautiful sight it was ! Villages, hamlets, large farms, towers, steeples, fields, meadows, orchards, and very fine timber trees, scattered all over the valley. The shape of the thing is this : on each side *downs*, very lofty and steep in some places, and sloping miles back in other places ; but each
10 *out-side* of the valley are downs. From the edge of the downs begin capital *arable fields* generally of very great dimensions, and, in some places, running a mile or two back into little *cross-valleys*, formed by hills of downs. After the corn-fields come *meadows* on each side, down to the *brook* or *river*. The farm-houses, mansions, villages, and hamlets are generally situated in that part of the arable land which comes nearest the meadows. Great as my expectations had been, they were more than fulfilled. I delight in this sort of country ; and I had frequently
20 seen the vale of the Itchen, that of the Bourn, and also that of the Teste in Hampshire ; I had seen the vales amongst the South Downs ; but I never before saw anything to please me like this valley of the Avon. I sat upon my horse and looked over Milton and Easton and Pewsey for half an hour, though I had not breakfasted. . . .

The shelter in these valleys, and particularly where the downs are steep and lofty on the sides, is very complete. Then the trees are everywhere lofty. They are generally elms, with some ashes, which delight in the soil that they
30 find here. There are, almost always, two or three large clumps of trees in every parish, and a rookery or two (not *rag*-rookery) to every parish. By the water's edge there

are willows ; and to almost every farm there is a fine orchard, the trees being, in general, very fine, and this year they are, in general, well loaded with fruit. So that, all taken together, it seems impossible to find a more beautiful and pleasant country than this, or to imagine any life more easy and happy than men might here lead if they were untormented by an accursed system that takes the food from those that raise it, and gives it to those that do nothing that is useful to man.

Uphusband (Hurstbourn Tarrant) in Hampshire

(From *Rural Rides*, October 11, 1826.

THE houses of the village are in great part scattered 10 about, and are amongst very lofty and fine trees ; and from many, many points round about, from the hilly fields, now covered with the young wheat, or with scarcely less beautiful sainfoin, the village is a sight worth going many miles to see. The lands, too, are pretty beyond description. These chains of hills make, below them, an endless number of lower hills, of varying shapes and sizes and aspects and of relative state as to each other ; while the surface presents in the size and form of the fields, in the woods, the hedge-rows, the sainfoin, the young wheat, the turnips, the tares, 20 the fallows, the sheep-folds and the flocks, and at every turn of your head a fresh and different set of these ; this surface all together presents that which I, at any rate, could look at with pleasure for ever. Not a sort of country that I like so well as when there are *downs* and a *broader valley* and *more of meadow ;* but a sort of country that I like next to that ; for here, as there, there are no ditches, no water-furrows, no dirt, and never any drought to cause inconvenience. The chalk is at bottom, and it takes care of all. 30

Southampton Water

(From *Rural Rides*, October 18, 1826.)

THE Southampton Water begins at Portsmouth, and goes up by Southampton to Redbridge, being, upon an average, about two miles wide, having on the one side the New Forest and on the other side, for a great part of the way, this fine and beautiful estate of Mr. Chamberlayne. Both sides of this water have rising lands divided into hill and dale, and very beautifully clothed with trees, the woods and lawns and fields being most advantageously intermixed. It is very curious that, at the *back* of each of these tracts
10 of land, there are extensive heaths, on this side as well as on the New Forest side. To stand here and look across the water at the New Forest, you would imagine that it was really *a country of woods ;* for you can see nothing of the heaths from here ; those heaths over which we rode, and from which we could see a windmill down among the trees, which windmill is now to be seen just opposite this place. So that the views from this place are the most beautiful that can be imagined. You see up the water and down the water, to Redbridge one way and out to Spithead
20 the other way. Through the trees, to the right, you see the spires of Southampton, and you have only to walk a mile, over a beautiful lawn and through a not less beautiful wood, to find, in a little dell, surrounded with lofty woods, the venerable ruins of *Netley Abbey*, which make part of Mr. Chamberlayne's estate.

The woods here are chiefly of oak ; the ground consists of a series of hill and dale, as you go long-wise from one end of the estate to the other, *about six miles in length.* Down almost every little valley that divides these hills or
30 hillocks there is more or less of water, making the under-wood, in those parts, very thick and dark to go through ; and these form the most delightful contrast with the fields

and lawns. There are innumerable vessels of various sizes continually upon the water ; and to those that delight in water-scenes this is certainly the very prettiest place that I ever saw in my life.

At Selborne

(From *Rural Rides*, August 7, 1823.)

As I was coming into this village, I observed to a farmer who was standing at his gateway, that people ought to be happy here, for that God had done everything for them. His answer was, that he did not believe there was a more unhappy place in England : for that there were always quarrels of some sort or other going on.   10

Hawkley Hanger in Hampshire

(From *Rural Rides*, November 24, 1822.)

At Bower I got instructions to go to Hawkley, but accompanied with most earnest advice not to go that way, for that it was impossible to get along. The roads were represented as so bad ; the floods so much out ; the hills and bogs so dangerous ; that, really, I began to *doubt ;* and, if I had not been brought up amongst the clays of the Holt Forest and the bogs of the neighbouring heaths, I should certainly have turned off to my right, to go over Hindhead, great as was my objection to going that way. 'Well, then,' said my friend at Bower, 'if you *will* go that 20 way, by G—, you must go down *Hawkley Hanger ;*' of which he then gave me *such* a description ! But even this I found to fall short of the reality. I inquired simply, whether *people were in the habit* of going down it ; and the answer being in the affirmative, on I went through green lanes and bridle-ways till I came to the turnpike-road from Petersfield to Winchester, which I crossed, going into a narrow and almost untrodden green lane, on the side of which I found a cottage. Upon my asking the way to *Hawkley*, the woman at the cottage said, ' Right up the lane, sir : you'll come to a *hanger* presently : you must take care, sir : you can't ride down : will your horses *go alone?* '

On we trotted up this pretty green lane ; and indeed, we had been coming gently and generally uphill for a good while. The lane was between highish banks and pretty high stuff growing on the banks, so that we could see no distance from us, and could receive not the smallest hint
10 of what was so near at hand. The lane had a little turn towards the end ; so that, out we came, all in a moment, at the very edge of the hanger ! And never, in all my life, was I so surprised and so delighted ! I pulled up my horse, and sat and looked ; and it was like looking from the top of a castle down into the sea, except that the valley was land and not water. I looked at my servant, to see what effect this unexpected sight had upon him. His surprise was as great as mine, though he had been bred amongst the North Hampshire hills. Those who had
20 so strenuously dwelt on the dirt and dangers of this route, had said not a word about beauties, the matchless beauties of the scenery. These hangers are woods on the sides of very steep hills. The trees and underwood *hang*, in some sort, to the ground, instead of *standing on* it. Hence these places are called *Hangers*. From the summit of that which I had now to descend, I looked down upon the villages of Hawkley, Greatham, Selborne and some others.

From the south-east, round, southward, to the north-west, the main valley has cross-valleys running out of it,
30 the hills on the sides of which are very steep, and, in many parts, covered with wood. The hills that form these cross-valleys run out into the main valley, like piers into the sea. Two of these promontories, of great height, are on the west side of the main valley, and were the first objects that struck my sight when I came to the edge of the hanger,

which was on the south. The ends of these promontories
are nearly perpendicular, and their tops so high in the air,
that you cannot look at the village below without something
like a feeling of apprehension. The leaves are all off, the
hop-poles are in stack, the fields have little verdure ; but,
while the spot is beautiful beyond description even now,
I must leave to imagination to suppose what it is when
the trees and hangers and hedges are in leaf, the corn
waving, the meadows bright, and the hops upon the poles !

From the south-west, round, eastward, to the north, lie 10
the *healhs*, of which Woolmer Forest makes a part, and
these go gradually rising up to Hindhead, the crown of
which is to the north-west, leaving the rest of the circle
(the part from north to north-west) to be occupied by
a continuation of the valley towards Headley, Binstead,
Frensham and the Holt Forest. So that even the *contrast*
in the view from the top of the hanger is as great as can
possibly be imagined. Men, however, are not to have such
beautiful views as this without some trouble. We had had
the view ; but we had to go down the hanger. We had, 20
indeed, some roads to get along, as we could, afterwards ;
but we had to get down the hanger first. The horses took
the lead, and crept partly down upon their feet and partly
upon their hocks. It was extremely slippery too ; for the
soil is a sort of marl, or, as they call it here, maume, or
mame, which is, when wet, very much like *grey soap*. In
such a case it was likely that I should keep in the rear,
which I did, and I descended by taking hold of the branches
of the underwood, and so letting myself down. When we
got to the bottom, I bade my man, when he should go 30
back to Uphusband, tell the people there that *Ashmansworth
Lane* is not the *worst* piece of road in the world. Our worst,
however, was not come yet, nor had we by any means seen
the most novel sights.

After crossing a little field and going through a farmyard,

we came into a lane, which was, at once, road and river.
We found a hard bottom, however ; and when we got out
of the water, we got into a lane with high banks.   The
banks were quarries of white stone, like Portland stone,
and the bed of the road was of the same stone ; and, the
rains having been heavy for a day or two before, the whole
was as clean and as white as the steps of a fundholder or
dead-weight doorway in one of the squares of the *Wen.*
Here were we, then, going along a stone road with stone
10 banks, and yet the underwood and trees grew well upon
the tops of the banks.   In the solid stone beneath us, there
were a horse-track and wheel-tracks, the former about
three and the latter about six inches deep.   How many
many ages it must have taken the horses' feet, the wheels,
and the water, to wear down this stone so as to form
a hollow way !   The horses seemed alarmed at their situation ; they trod with fear ; but they took us along very
nicely, and, at last, got us safe into the indescribable dirt
and mire of the road from Hawkley Green to Greatham.
20 Here the bottom of all the land is this solid white stone,
and the top is that *mame*, which I have before described.
The hop-roots penetrate down into this stone.   How deep
the stone may go I know not ; but, when I came to look
up at the end of one of the piers, or promontories, mentioned
above, I found that it was all of this same stone.

A Garden at Burghclere in Hampshire

(From *Rural Rides*, October 30, 1821.)

CAME through a place called ' a park ' belonging to
a Mr. Montague, who is now *abroad ;* for the purpose,
I suppose, of generously assisting to compensate the French
people for what they lost by the entrance of the Holy
30 Alliance Armies into their country.   Of all the ridiculous
things I ever saw in my life this place is the most ridiculous.

The house looks like a sort of church, in somewhat of
a gothic style of building, with *crosses* on the tops of
different parts of the pile. There is a sort of swamp, at
the foot of a wood, at no great distance from the front of
the house. This swamp has been dug out in the middle
to show the water to the eye ; so that there is a sort of
river, or chain of diminutive lakes, going down a little
valley, about 500 yards long, the water proceeding from
the *soak* of the higher ground on both sides. By the sides
of these lakes there are little flower gardens, laid out in
the Dutch manner ; that is to say, cut out into all manner
of superficial geometrical figures. Here is the *grand en
petit*, or mock magnificence, more complete than I ever
beheld it before. Here is a *fountain*, the basin of which is
not four feet over, and the water spout not exceeding the
pour from a tea-pot. Here is a *bridge* over a *river* of which
a child four years old would clear the banks at a jump.
I could not have trusted myself on the bridge for fear of
the consequences to Mr. Montague ; but I very conveniently
stepped over the river, in imitation of the *Colossus*. In
another part there was a *lion's mouth* spouting out water
into the lake, which was so much like the vomiting of a dog,
that I could almost have pitied the poor Lion. In short,
such fooleries I never before beheld ; but what I disliked
most was the apparent impiety of a part of these works of
refined taste. I did not like the crosses on the dwelling
house ; but, in one of the gravel walks, we had to pass
under a gothic arch, with a cross on the top of it, and in
the point of the arch a niche for a saint or a virgin, the
figure being gone through the lapse of centuries, and the
pedestal only remaining as we so frequently see on the
outsides of Cathedrals and of old churches and chapels.
But the good of it was, this gothic arch, disfigured by the
hand of old Father Time, was composed of Scotch fir wood,
as rotten as a pear ; nailed together in such a way as to

make the thing appear, from a distance, like the remnant of a ruin! I wonder how long this sickly, this childish, taste is to remain? I do not know who this gentleman is. I suppose he is some honest person from the 'Change or its neighbourhood; and that these *gothic arches* are to denote the *antiquity of his origin!* Not a bad plan; and, indeed, it is one that I once took the liberty to recommend to those Fundlords who retire to be country-'squires. But I never recommended the *Crucifixes!* To be sure the Roman Catholic religion may, in England, be considered as a *gentleman's religion*, it being the most *ancient* in the country; and, therefore, it is fortunate for a Fundlord when he happens (if he ever do happen) to be of that faith.

This gentleman may, for anything that I know, be a *Catholic;* in which case I applaud his piety and pity his taste. At the end of this scene of mock grandeur and mock antiquity I found something more rational; namely, some hare hounds, and, in half-an-hour after, we found, and I had the first hare-hunt that I had had since I wore a smock-frock! We killed our hare after good sport, and got to Burghclere in the evening to a nice farm-house in a dell, sheltered from every wind, and with plenty of good living; though with no gothic arches made of Scotch-fir!

A Garden in Surrey

(From *Rural Rides*, November 30, 1822.)

ALBURY is a little village consisting of a few houses, with a large house or two near it. At the end of the village we came to a park, which is the residence of Mr. Drummond. —Having heard a great deal of this park, and of the gardens, I wished very much to see them. My way to Dorking lay through Shire, and it went along on the outside of the park. I *guessed*, as the Yankees say, that there must

be a way through the park to Shire ; and I fell upon the
scheme of going into the park as far as Mr. Drummond's
house, and then asking his leave to go out at the other
end of it. This scheme, though pretty barefaced, succeeded
very well. It is true that I was aware that I had not
a *Norman* to deal with ; or I should not have ventured
upon the experiment. I sent in word that, having got
into the park, I should be exceedingly obliged to Mr. Drummond if he would let me go out of it on the side next to
Shire. He not only granted this request, but, in the most 10
obliging manner, permitted us to ride all about the park,
and to see his gardens, which, without any exception, are,
to my fancy, the prettiest in England ; that is to say, that
I ever saw in England.

They say that these gardens were laid out for one of the
Howards, in the reign of Charles the Second, by Mr. Evelyn,
who wrote the *Sylva*. The mansion-house, which is by no
means magnificent, stands on a little flat by the side of the
parish church, having a steep, but not lofty, hill rising up
on the south side of it. It looks right across the gardens, 20
which lie on the slope of a hill which runs along at about
a quarter of a mile distant from the front of the house.
The gardens, of course, lie facing the south. At the back
of them, under the hill, is a high wall ; and there is also
a wall at each end, running from north to south. Between
the house and the gardens there is a very beautiful run of
water, with a sort of little wild narrow sedgy meadow.
The gardens are separated from this by a hedge, running
along from east to west. From this hedge there go up the
hill, at right angles, several other hedges, which divide 30
the land here into distinct gardens, or orchards. Along
at the top of these there goes a yew hedge, or, rather,
a row of small yew trees, the trunks of which are bare for
about eight or ten feet high, and the tops of which form
one solid head of about ten feet high, while the bottom

branches come out on each side of the row about eight
feet horizontally. This hedge, or row, is *a quarter of a mile
long*. There is a nice hard sand-road under this species
of umbrella ; and, summer and winter, here is a most
delightful walk ! Behind this row of yews there is a space,
or garden (a quarter of a mile long you will observe), about
thirty or forty feet wide, as nearly as I can recollect. At
the back of this garden, and facing the yew-tree row, is
a wall probably ten feet high, which forms the breastwork
10 of a *terrace ;* and it is this terrace which is the most beautiful
thing that I ever saw in the gardening way. It is a quarter
of a mile long, and, I believe, between thirty and forty feet
wide ; of the finest green sward, and as level as a die.

The wall, along at the back of this terrace, stands close
against the hill, which you see with the trees and underwood upon it rising above the wall. So that here is the
finest spot for fruit trees that can possibly be imagined.
At both ends of this garden the trees in the park are lofty,
and there are a pretty many of them. The hills on the
20 south side of the mansion-house are covered with lofty
trees, chiefly beeches and chestnut : so that a warmer,
a more sheltered, spot than this, it seems to be impossible
to imagine. Observe, too, how judicious it was to plant
the row of yew trees at the distance which I have described
from the wall which forms the breastwork of the terrace :
that wall, as well as the wall at the back of the terrace,
are covered with fruit trees, and the yew-tree row is just
high enough to defend the former from winds, without
injuring it by its shade. In the middle of the wall, at the
30 back of the terrace, there is a recess, about thirty feet in
front and twenty feet deep, and here is a *basin*, into which
rises a spring coming out of the hill. The overflowings of
this basin go under the terrace and down across the garden
into the rivulet below. So that here is water at the top,
across the middle, and along at the bottom of this garden.

Take it altogether, this, certainly, is the prettiest garden
that I ever beheld. There was taste and sound judgment
at every step in the laying out of this place. Everywhere
utility and convenience is combined with beauty. The
terrace is by far the finest thing of the sort that I ever saw,
and the whole thing altogether is a great compliment to the
taste of the times in which it was formed. I know there
are some ill-natured persons who will say that I want
a revolution that would turn Mr. Drummond out of this
place and put me into it. Such persons will hardly believe 10
me, but upon my word I do not. From everything that
I hear, Mr. Drummond is very worthy of possessing it
himself, seeing that he is famed for his justice and his
kindness *towards the labouring classes*, who, God knows,
have very few friends amongst the rich.

The Woodlands of Sussex

(From *Rural Rides*, January 2, 1822.)

THE agricultural state of the country or, rather, the
quality of the land, from Bromley to Battle, may be judged
of from the fact that I did not see, as I came along, more
than thirty acres of swedes during the fifty-six miles ! In 20
Norfolk I should, in the same distance, have seen five
hundred acres ! However, man was not the maker of the
land ; and, as to human happiness, I am of opinion that as
much, and even more, falls to the lot of the leather-legged
chaps that live in and rove about amongst those clays and
woods as to the more regularly disciplined labourers of the
rich and prime parts of England. As ' God has made the
back to the burthen,' so the clay and coppice people make
the dress to the stubs and bushes. Under the sole of the
shoe is *iron ;* from the sole six inches upwards is a high- 30
low ; then comes a leather bam to the knee ; then comes
a pair of leather breeches ; then comes a stout doublet ;

over this comes a smock-frock ; and the wearer sets brush and stubs and thorns and mire at defiance. I have always observed that woodland and forest labourers are best off in the main. The coppices give them pleasant and profitable work in winter. If they have not so great a corn-harvest, they have a three weeks' harvest in April or May ; that is to say, in the season of barking, which in Hampshire is called *stripping*, and in Sussex *flaying*, which employs women and children as well as men. And then in the great
10 article of *fuel !* They *buy* none. It is miserable work where this is to be bought, and where, as at Salisbury, the poor take by turns the making of fires at their houses to boil four or five tea-kettles. . . .

Woodland countries are interesting on many accounts. Not so much on account of their masses of green leaves, as on account of the variety of sights and sounds and incidents that they afford. Even in winter the coppices are beautiful to the eye, while they comfort the mind with the idea of shelter and warmth. In spring they change their hue
20 from day to day during two whole months, which is about the time from the first appearance of the delicate leaves of the birch to the full expansion of those of the ash ; and even before the leaves come at all to intercept the view, what in the vegetable creation is so delightful to behold as the bed of a coppice bespangled with primroses and blue-bells ? The opening of the birch leaves is the signal for the pheasant to begin to crow, for the blackbird to whistle, and the thrush to sing ; and just when the oak-buds begin to look reddish, and not a day before, the whole tribe of
30 finches burst forth in songs from every bough, while the lark, imitating them all, carries the joyous sounds to the sky. These are amongst the means which Providence has benignantly appointed to sweeten the toils by which food and raiment are produced ; these the English Ploughman could once hear without the sorrowful reflection that he

himself was *a pauper*, and that the bounties of nature had, for him, been scattered in vain !

The Park at Petworth, Sussex

(From *Rural Rides*, November 13, 1825.)

To our great delight we found Richard's horse quite well this morning, and off we set for this place. The first part of our road, for about three miles and a half, was through Lord Egremont's park. The morning was very fine ; the sun shining ; a sharp frost after a foggy evening ; the grass all white, the twigs of the trees white, the ponds frozen over ; and everything looking exceedingly beautiful. The spot itself being one of the very finest in the world, not excepting, I dare say, that of the father of Saxe Coburg itself, who has, doubtless, many such fine places.

In a very fine pond, not far from the house and close by the road, there are some little artificial islands, upon one of which I observed an arbutus loaded with its beautiful fruit (quite ripe) even more thickly than any one I ever saw even in America. There were, on the side of the pond, a most numerous and beautiful collection of water-fowl, foreign as well as domestic. I never saw so great a variety of water-fowl collected together in my life. They had been ejected from the water by the frost, and were sitting apparently in a state of great dejection : but this circumstance had brought them into a comparatively small compass ; and we facing our horses about, sat and looked at them, at the pond, at the grass, at the house, till we were tired of admiring. Everything here is in the neatest and most beautiful state. Endless herds of deer, of all the varieties of colours ; and what adds greatly to your pleasure in such a case, you see comfortable retreats prepared for them in different parts of the woods. When we came to what we thought the end of the park, the gate-keeper told

us that we should find other walls to pass through. We now entered upon woods, we then came to another wall, and there we entered upon farms to our right and to our left. At last we came to a third wall, and the gate in that let us out into the turnpike-road. The gate-keeper here told us that the whole enclosure was *nine miles round ;* and this, after all, forms, probably, not a quarter part of what this nobleman possesses. And is it wrong that one man should possess so much ? By no means ; but in my
10 opinion it is wrong that a system should exist which compels this man to have his estate taken away from him unless he throw the junior branches of his family for maintenance upon the public.

The Weald of Kent

(From *Rural Rides*, September 6, 1823.)

I HAVE now, in order to get to the Wen, to cross the chalk-ridge once more, and at a point where I never crossed it before. Coming through the Weald I found the corn very good ; and low as the ground is, wet as it is, cold as it is, there will be very little of the wheat which will not be housed before Saturday night. All the corn is good,
20 and the barley excellent. Not far from Bough-beach, I saw two oak trees, one of which was, they told me, more than thirty feet round, and the other more than twenty-seven ; but they have been hollow for half a century. They are not much bigger than the oak upon Tilford Green, if any. I mean in the trunk ; but they are hollow, while that tree is sound in all its parts, and growing still. I have had a most beautiful ride through the Weald. The day is very hot ; but I have been in the shade ; and my horse's feet very often in the rivulets and wet lanes. In
30 one place I rode above a mile completely arched over by

the boughs of the underwood, growing in the banks of the lane. What an odd taste that man must have who prefers a turnpike-road to a lane like this.

At Sittingbourne

(From *Rural Rides*, December 5, 1821.)

THIS is a country of hop-gardens, cherry, apple, pear and filbert orchards, and quickset hedges. But, alas ! what, in point of *beauty*, is a country without woods and lofty trees ! And here there are very few indeed. I am now sitting in a room, from the window of which I look, *first*, over a large and level field of rich land, in which the drilled wheat is finely come up, and which is surrounded 10 by clipped quickset hedges with a row of apple trees running by the sides of them ; *next*, over a long succession of rich meadows, which are here called marshes, the shortest grass upon which will fatten sheep or oxen ; *next*, over a little branch of the salt water which runs up to Faversham ; *beyond that*, on the Isle of Shepry (or Shepway), which rises a little into a sort of ridge that runs along it ; rich fields, pastures and orchards lie all around me ; and yet, I declare, that I a million times to one prefer, as a spot to *live on*, the heaths, the miry coppices, the wild woods and the forests 20 of Sussex and Hampshire.

The Corn-fields of Hertfordshire

(From *Rural Rides*, June 24, 1822.)

THE *trees* from Redbourn to Hempstead are very fine ; oaks, ashes, and beeches. Some of the finest of each sort, and the very finest ashes I ever saw in my life. They are in great numbers, and make the fields look most beautiful. No villainous things of the *fir-tribe* offend the eye here. The custom is in this part of Hertfordshire (and I am told

it continues into Bedfordshire) to leave a *border* round the
ploughed part of the fields to bear grass and to make hay
from, so that, the grass being now made into hay, every
corn field has a closely mowed grass walk about ten feet
wide all round it, between the corn and the hedge. This
is most beautiful ! The hedges are now full of the shepherd's
rose, honeysuckles, and all sorts of wild flowers ; so that
you are upon a grass walk, with this most beautiful of all
flower gardens and shrubberies on your one hand, and
10 with the corn on the other. And thus you go from field
to field (on foot or on horseback), the sort of corn, the sort
of underwood and timber, the shape and size of the fields,
the height of the hedge-rows, the height of the trees, all
continually varying. Talk of *pleasure-grounds* indeed !
What that man ever invented, under the name of pleasure-
grounds, can equal these fields in Hertfordshire ?

Huntingdon

(From *Rural Rides*, January 22, 1822.)

HUNTINGDON is a very clean and nice place, contains
many elegant houses, and the environs are beautiful.
Above and below the bridge, under which the Ouse passes,
20 are the most beautiful, and by far the most beautiful,
meadows that I ever saw in my life. The meadows at
Lewes, at Guildford, at Farnham, at Winchester, at
Salisbury, at Exeter, at Gloucester, at Hereford, and even
at Canterbury, are nothing, compared with those of
Huntingdon in point of beauty. Here are no reeds, here
is no sedge, no unevennesses of any sort. Here are *bowling-
greens* of hundreds of acres in extent, with a river winding
through them, full to the brink. *One* of these meadows
is the *race-course ;* and so pretty a spot, so level, so smooth,
30 so green, and of such an extent I never saw, and never
expected to see. From the bridge you look across the

valleys, first to the west and then to the east ; the valleys
terminate at the foot of rising ground, well set with trees,
from amongst which church spires raise their heads here
and there. I think it would be very difficult to find a more
delightful spot than this in the world.

Suffolk ; and the Southern Counties

(From *Rural Rides*, March 22, 1830.)

COMING from Ipswich to Bury St. Edmund's, you pass
through Needham Market and Stowmarket, two very pretty
market towns ; and, like all the other towns in Suffolk, free
from the drawback of shabby and beggarly houses on the
outskirts. I remarked that I did not see in the whole 10
county one single instance of paper or rags supplying the
place of glass in any window, and did not see one miserable
hovel in which a labourer resided. The county, however,
is *flat :* with the exception of the environs of Ipswich, there
is none of that beautiful variety of hill and dale and hanging
woods that you see at every town in Hampshire, Sussex,
and Kent. It is curious, too, that though the people,
I mean the poorer classes of people, are extremely neat in
their houses, and though I found all their gardens dug up
and prepared for cropping, you do not see about their 20
cottages (and it is just the same in Norfolk) that *ornamental
gardening ;* the walks, and the flower borders, and the
honeysuckles and roses trained over the doors or over
arched sticks, that you see in Hampshire, Sussex, and
Kent, that I have many a time sitten upon my horse to
look at so long and so often, as greatly to retard me on
my journey. Nor is this done for show or ostentation.
If you find a cottage in those counties, by the side of
a *by lane,* or in the midst of a forest, you find just the
same care about the garden and the flowers. In those 30
counties, too, there is great taste with regard *to trees* of every

description, from the hazel to the oak. In Suffolk it appears
to be just the contrary : here is the great dissight of all
these three eastern counties. Almost every bank of every
field is studded with *pollards*, that is to say, trees that
have been *beheaded*, at from six to twelve feet from the
ground, than which nothing in nature can be more ugly.

That which we *admire* most is not always that which
would be *our choice*. One might imagine that after
all that I have said about this fine county, I should
10 certainly prefer it as a place of residence. I should not,
however : my choice has been always very much divided
between the woods of Sussex and the downs of Wiltshire.
I should not like to be compelled to decide : but if I were
compelled, I do believe that I should fix on some vale
in Wiltshire. Water meadows at the bottom, corn-land
going up towards the hills, those hills being *down land*,
and a farmhouse, in a clump of trees, in some little cross
vale between the hills, sheltered on every side but the
south. In short, if Mr. Bennet would give me a farm, the
20 house of which lies on the right-hand side of the road going
from Salisbury to Warminster, in the parish of Norton
Bovant, just before you enter that village ; if he would
but be so good as to do that, I would freely give up all
the rest of the world to the possession of whoever may
get hold of it. I have hinted this to him once or twice
before, but I am sorry to say that he turns a deaf ear to
my hinting.

The Fens

(From *Rural Rides*, April 9, 1830.)

To Crowland I went, as before stated, from Wisbeach,
staying two nights at St. Edmund's. Here I was in the
30 heart of the Fens. The whole country as *level* as the table
on which I am now writing. The horizon like the sea in
a dead calm : you see the morning sun come up just as

at sea ; and see it go down over the rim in just the same
way as at sea in a calm. The land covered with beautiful
grass, with sheep lying about upon it as fat as hogs stretched
out sleeping in a stye. The kind and polite friends with
whom we were lodged had a very neat garden and fine young
orchard. Everything grows well here : earth without
a stone so big as a pin's head ; grass as thick as it can
grow on the ground ; immense bowling-greens separated
by ditches ; and not the sign of dock or thistle or other
weed to be seen. What a contrast between these and the 10
heath-covered sand-hills of Surrey, amongst which I was
born ! Yet the labourers, who spuddle about the ground
in the little *dips* between those sand-hills, are better off
than those that exist in this fat of the land. *Here* the
grasping system takes *all* away, because it has the means
of coming at the value of all : *there*, the poor man enjoys
something, because he is thought too poor to have anything :
he is there allowed to have what is deemed *worth nothing* ;
but here, where every inch is valuable, not one inch is he
permitted to enjoy.   20

Lincolnshire

(From *Rural Rides*, April 13, 1830.)

THERE is one deficiency, and that, with me, a great one,
throughout this country of corn and grass and oxen and
sheep, that I have come over during the last three weeks ;
namely, the want of *singing birds*. We are now just in
that season when they sing most. Here, in all this country,
I have seen and heard only about four sky-larks, and not
one other singing bird of any description, and of the small
birds that do not sing I have seen only one *yellowhammer*,
and it was perched on the rail of a pound between Boston
and Sibsey. Oh ! the thousands of linnets all singing 30
together on one tree in the sand-hills of Surrey ! Oh !
the carolling in the coppices and the dingles of Hampshire

and Sussex and Kent ! At this moment (5 o'clock in the morning) the groves at Barn-Elm are echoing with the warblings of thousands upon thousands of birds. The *thrush* begins a little before it is light ; next the *blackbird* ; next the *larks* begin to rise ; all the rest begin the moment the sun gives the signal ; and from the hedges, the bushes, from the middle and the topmost twigs of the trees, comes the singing of endless variety ; from the long dead grass comes the sound of the sweet and soft voice of the *white-*
10 *throat* or *nettle-tom*, while the loud and merry song of the *lark* (the songster himself out of sight) seems to descend from the skies. Milton, in his description of paradise, has not omitted the ' song of earliest birds.' However, everything taken together, here, in Lincolnshire, are more good things than man could have had the conscience to *ask* of God.

Yorkshire and Yorkshiremen

(From *Rural Rides*, April 19, 1830.)

THE country round Hull appears to exceed even that of Lincolnshire. The three mornings that I was at Hull I walked out in three different directions, and found the
20 country everywhere fine. To the east lies the Holderness country. I used to wonder that Yorkshire, to which I, from some false impression in my youth, had always attached the idea of *sterility*, should send us of the south those beautiful cattle with short horns and straight and deep bodies. You have only to see the country to cease to wonder at this. It lies on the north side of the mouth of the Humber ; is as flat and fat as the land between Holbeach and Boston, without, as they tell me, the necessity of such numerous ditches. The appellation
30 ' Yorkshire *bite* ; ' the acute sayings ascribed to Yorkshiremen ; and their quick manner I remember in the army. When speaking of what country a man was, one used to

say, in defence of the party, ' York, but honest.' Another saying was, that it was a bare common that a Yorkshireman would go over without taking a bite. Every one knows the story of the gentleman who, upon finding that a boot-cleaner in the south was a Yorkshireman, and expressing his surprise that he was not become master of the inn, received for answer, ' Ah, sir, but master is York too ! ' And that of the Yorkshire boy who, seeing a gentleman eating some eggs, asked the cook to give him a little *salt* ; and upon being asked what he could want with salt, he 10 said, ' perhaps that gentleman may give me an egg presently.'

It is surprising what effect sayings like these produce upon the mind. From one end to the other of the kingdom Yorkshiremen are looked upon as being keener than other people ; more eager in pursuit of their own interests ; more sharp and more selfish. For my part, I was cured with regard to the *people* long before I saw Yorkshire. In the army, where we see men of all counties, I always found Yorkshiremen distinguished for their frank manners and 20 generous disposition.

Hare-hunting ; at Orcop, Herefordshire

(From *Rural Rides*, November 16, 1821.)

A WHOLE day most delightfully passed a hare-hunting, with a pretty pack of hounds kept here by Messrs. Palmer. They put me upon a horse that seemed to have been made on purpose for me, strong, tall, gentle and bold ; and that carried me either over or through everything. I, who am just the weight of a four-bushel sack of good wheat, actually sat on his back from daylight in the morning to dusk (about nine hours), without once setting my foot on the ground. Our ground was at Orcop, a place about four 30 miles distance from this place. We found a hare in a few minutes after throwing off ; and in the course of the day,

we had to find four, and were never more than ten minutes in finding. A steep and naked ridge, lying between two flat valleys, having a mixture of pretty large fields and small woods, formed our ground. The hares crossed the ridge forward and backward, and gave us numerous views and very fine sport.—I never rode on such steep ground before ; and, really, in going up and down some of the craggy places, where the rains had washed the earth from the rocks, I did think, once or twice, of my neck, and how
10 Sidmouth would like to see me.

Bredon Hill, Worcestershire

(From *Rural Rides*, September 25, 1826.)

FROM Bredon Hill you see into nine or ten counties ; and those curious bubblings-up, the Malvern Hills, are right before you, and only at about ten miles' distance, in a straight line. As this hill looks over the counties of Worcester, Gloucester, Hereford and part of Warwick and the rich part of Stafford ; and as it looks over the vales of Esham, Worcester, and Gloucester, having the Avon and the Severn winding down them, you certainly see from this Bredon Hill one of the very richest spots of England,
20 and I am fully convinced a richer spot than is to be seen in any other country in the world ; I mean *Scotland excepted*, of course, for fear Sawney should cut my throat, or, which is much the same thing, squeeze me by the hand, from which last I pray thee to deliver me, O Lord !

Guildford

(From *Rural Rides*, October 13, 1825.)

WE set out from Chilworth to-day about noon. This is a little hamlet, lying under the south side of St. Martha's Hill ; and on the other side of that hill, a little to the north-west, is the town of Guildford, which (taken with its environs) I, who have seen so many, many towns, think the prettiest, and, taken all together, the most agreeable and most happy-looking that I ever saw in my life. Here are hill and dell in endless variety. Here are the chalk and the sand, vieing with each other in making beautiful scenes. Here is a navigable river and fine meadows. Here are woods and downs. Here is something of everything but *fat marshes* and their skeleton-making *agues*. The vale, all the way down to Chilworth from Reigate, is very delightful. 10

At Salisbury

(From *Rural Rides*, August 21, 1826.)

FOR my part, I could not look up at the spire and the whole of the church at Salisbury without feeling that I lived in degenerate times. Such a thing never could be made *now*. We *feel* that, as we look at the building. It really does appear that if our forefathers had not made these buildings we should have forgotten, before now, what the Christian religion was !

Malmesbury

(From *Rural Rides*, September 11, 1826.)

THIS town, though it has nothing particularly engaging in itself, stands upon one of the prettiest spots that can be imagined. Besides the river Avon, which I went down in 20 the south-east part of the country, here is another river Avon, which runs down to Bath, and two branches, or sources, of which meet here. There is a pretty ridge of ground, the base of which is a mile or a mile and a half wide. On each side of this ridge a branch of the river runs down, through a flat of very fine meadows. The town and the beautiful remains of the famous old abbey stand on the rounded spot which terminates this ridge ; and, just

below, nearly close to the town, the two branches of the
river meet ; and then they begin to be called *the Avon*.
The land round about is excellent, and of a great variety
of forms. The trees are lofty and fine : so that what with
the water, the meadows, the fine cattle and sheep, and, as
I hear, the absence of *hard*-pinching poverty, this is a very
pleasant place. There remains more of the abbey than,
I believe, of any of our monastic buildings, except that of
Westminster, and those that have become cathedrals. The
10 church service is performed in the part of the abbey that
is left standing. The parish church has fallen down and
is gone ; but the tower remains, which is made use of for
the bells; but the abbey is used as the church, though the
church-tower is at a considerable distance from it. It was
once a most magnificent building ; and there is now a *doorway* which is the most beautiful thing I ever saw, and which
was, nevertheless, built in Saxon times, in ' the *dark* ages.'
. . .—What *fools*, as well as ungrateful creatures, we have
been and are ! There is a broken arch, standing off from
20 the sound part of the building, at which one cannot look
up without feeling shame at the thought of ever having
abused the men who made it. No one need *tell* any man
of sense ; he *feels* our inferiority to our fathers upon merely
beholding the remains of their efforts to ornament their
country and elevate the minds of the people.

Ipswich

(From *Rural Rides*, March 22, 1830.)

THERE is no doubt but that this was a much greater
place than it is now. It is the great outlet for the immense
quantities of corn grown in this most productive country,
and by farmers the most clever that ever lived. I am told
30 that wheat is worth six shillings a quarter more, at some
times, at Ipswich than at Norwich, the navigation to

London being so much more speedy and safe. Immense
quantities of flour are sent from this town. The windmills
on the hills in the vicinage are so numerous that I counted,
whilst standing in one place, no less than seventeen. They
are all painted or washed white ; the sails are black ; it
was a fine morning, the wind was brisk, and their twirling
altogether added greatly to the beauty of the scene, which,
having the broad and beautiful arm of the sea on the one
hand, and the fields and meadows, studded with farm-
houses, on the other, appeared to me the most beautiful 10
sight of the kind that I had ever beheld. The town and
its churches were down in the dell before me, and the only
object that came to disfigure the scene was the BARRACK,
and made me utter involuntarily the words of Blackstone :
' The laws of England recognise no distinction between
the citizen and the soldier ; they know of no standing
soldier ; no inland fortresses ; no barracks.' ' Ah ! ' said
I myself, but loud enough for any one to have heard me
a hundred yards, ' such *were* the laws of England when
mass was said in those magnificent churches, and such 20
they continued until a *septennial* parliament came and
deprived the people of England of their rights.'

I know of no town to be compared with Ipswich, except
it be Nottingham ; and there is this difference in the two ;
that Nottingham stands high and, on one side, looks over
a very fine country ; whereas Ipswich is in a dell, meadows
running up above it, and a beautiful arm of the sea below
it.   The town itself is substantially built, well paved,
everything good and solid, and no wretched dwellings to
be seen on its outskirts. From the town itself you can see 30
nothing ; but you can, in no direction, go from it a quarter
of a mile without finding views that a painter might crave,
and then the country round about it so well cultivated ;
the land in such a beautiful state, the farmhouses all white,
and all so much alike ; the barns, and everything about

the homesteads so snug ; the stocks of turnips so abundant everywhere ; the sheep and cattle in such fine order ; the wheat all drilled ; the ploughman so expert ; the furrows, if a quarter of a mile long, as straight as a line, and laid as truly as if with a level : in short, here is everything to delight the eye, and to make the people proud of their country ; and this is the case throughout the whole of this county. I have always found Suffolk farmers great boasters of their superiority over others ; and I must say that it is 10 not without reason.

Boston Stump

(From *Rural Rides*, April 11, 1830.)

THE great pride and glory of the Bostonians is *their church*, which is, I think, 400 feet long, 90 feet wide, and has a tower (or steeple, as they call it) 300 feet high, which is both a landmark and a sea-mark. To describe the rich-ness, the magnificence, the symmetry, the exquisite beauty of this pile is wholly out of my power. It is impossible to look at it without feeling, first, admiration and reverence and gratitude to the memory of our fathers who reared it ; and next, indignation at those who affect to believe, and 20 contempt for those who do believe, that when this pile was reared the age was *dark*, the people rude and ignorant, and the country *destitute of wealth* and *thinly peopled*. Look at this church, then look at the heaps of white rubbish that the parsons have lately stuck up under the ' *New-church Act*,' and which, after having been built with money forced from the nation by odious taxes, they have stuffed full of *locked-up pens*, called *pews* . . . nay, after having looked at this work of the ' *dark* ages,' look at that great, heavy, ugly, unmeaning mass of stone called St. Paul's . . . created 30 by a Protestant Parliament, and by taxes wrung by force from the whole nation ; and then say which is the age really meriting the epithet *dark*.

Hull

(From *Rural Rides*, April 19, 1820.)

NOR is the town of Hull itself to be overlooked. It is
a little city of London : streets, shops, everything like it ;
clean as the best parts of London, and the people as bustling
and attentive. The town of Hull is *surrounded* with com-
modious docks for shipping. These docks are separated, in
three or four places, by draw-bridges, so that, as you walk
round the town, you walk by the side of the docks and the
ships.   The town on the outside of the docks is pretty considerable, and the walks from it into the country beautiful. I
went about a good deal and I nowhere saw marks of beggary 10
or filth, even in the outskirts : none of those nasty, shabby,
thief-looking sheds that you see in the approaches to
London : none of those off-scourings of pernicious and
insolent luxury. I hate commercial towns in general :
there is generally something so loathsome in the look, and
so stern and unfeeling in the manners of sea-faring people,
that I have always, from my very youth, disliked sea-ports ;
but really, the sight of this nice town, the manners of its
people, the civil and kind and cordial reception that I met
with, and the clean streets, and especially the pretty 20
gardens in every direction, as you walk into the country,
has made Hull, though a sea-port, a place that I shall
always look back to with delight.

Oxford

(From *Rural Rides*, November 17, 1821.)

UPON beholding the masses of buildings, at Oxford,
devoted to what they call ' *learning*,' I could not help
reflecting on the drones that they contain and the wasps
they send forth ! However, malignant as some are, the

great and prevalent characteristic is *folly* : emptiness of head ; want of talent ; and one half of the fellows who are what they call *educated* here, are unfit to be clerks in a grocer's or mercer's shop.—As I looked up at what they call *University Hall*, I could not help reflecting that what I had written, even since I left Kensington on the 29th of October, would produce more effect, and do more good in the world, than all that had, for a hundred years, been written by all the members of this University . . . and
10 I could not help exclaiming to myself : ' Stand forth, ye big-wigged, ye gloriously feeding Doctors ! . . . Stand forth and face me, who have, from the pen of my leisure hours, sent amongst your flocks a hundred thousand sermons in ten months ! More than you have all done for the last half century ! ' I exclaimed in vain. I dare say (for it was at peep of day) that not a man of them had yet endeavoured to unclose his eyes.

Bristol

(From *Rural Rides*, July 3, 1830.)

BUT never shall I see another place to interest me, and so pleasing to me, as Bristol and its environs, taking the
20 whole together. A good and solid and wealthy city : a people of plain and good manners ; private virtue and public spirit united ; no empty noise, no insolence, no flattery ; men very much like the Yorkers and Lancastrians. And as to the seat of the city and its environs, it surpasses all that I ever saw. A great commercial city in the midst of corn-fields, meadows and woods, and the ships coming into the centre of it, miles from anything like sea, up a narrow river, and passing between two clefts of a rock probably a hundred feet high ; so that from the top of
30 these clefts you *look down* upon the main-topgallant masts of lofty ships that are gliding along !

THE STATE OF THE PEOPLE

Agricultural Wages

(From *Rural Rides*, November 12, 1825.)

AT about four miles from Petersfield we passed through a village called Rogate. Just before we came to it, I asked a man who was hedging on the side of the road how much he got a day. He said, 1s. 6d. : and he told me that the *allowed* wages was 7d. a day for the man *and a gallon loaf a week for the rest of his family* ; that is to say, one pound and two and a quarter ounces of bread for each of them ; and nothing more ! And this, observe, is one-third short of the bread allowance of gaols, to say nothing of the meat and clothing and lodging of the inhabitants of gaols. 10 If the man have full work ; if he get his eighteen-pence a day, the whole nine shillings does not purchase a gallon loaf each for a wife and three children, and two gallon loaves for himself.

In the Eastern Counties

(From *Rural Rides*, April 19, 1830 ; Spittal, near Lincoln.)

WITH regard to the labourers, they are, everywhere, miserable. The wages for those who are employed on the land are, through all the counties that I have come, twelve shillings a week for married men, and less for single ones ; but a large part of them are not even at this season employed on the land. The farmers, for want of means of profitable 20 employment, suffer the men to fall upon the parish ; and they are employed in digging and breaking stone for the roads ; so that the roads are nice and smooth for the sheep and cattle to walk on in their way to the all-devouring

jaws of the Jews and other tax-eaters in London and its
vicinity. None of the best meat, except by mere accident,
is consumed here. To-day (the 20th of April), we have
seen hundreds upon hundreds of sheep, as fat as hogs, go
by this inn door, their toes, like those of the foot-marks
at the entrance of the lion's den, all pointing towards the
Wen ; and the landlord gave us for dinner a little skinny
hard leg of old ewe mutton ! Where the man got it,
I cannot imagine. Thus it is : every good thing is literally
10 driven or carried away out of the country. In walking out
yesterday, I saw three poor fellows digging stone for the
roads, who told me that they never had anything but
bread to eat, and water to wash it down. One of them
was a widower with three children ; and his pay was
eighteenpence a day ; that is to say, about three pounds
of bread a day each, for six days in the week ; nothing for
Sunday, and nothing for lodging, washing, clothing, candle-
light, or fuel ! Just such was the state of things in France
at the eve of the Revolution !

The Farmers

(From *Rural Rides*, May 18, 1830.)

20   THUS have I come through countries of corn and meat
and iron and coal ; and from the banks of the Humber to
those of the Severn I find all the people who do not share
in the taxes in a state of distress, greater or less ; *mort-
gagers* all frightened out of their wits ; *fathers* trembling
for the fate of their children ; and *working people* in the
most miserable state, and, as they ought to be, in the
worst of temper. These will, I am afraid, be the *state-
doctors* at last ! The farmers are cowed down : the poorer
they get the more cowardly they are. Every one of them
30 sees the cause of his suffering, and sees general ruin at
hand ; but every one hopes that by some trick, some act

of meanness, some contrivance, *he shall escape.* So that
there is no hope of any change for the better but from the
working people. The farmers will sink to a very low state ;
and thus the Thing (barring *accidents*) may go on, until
neither farmer nor tradesman will see a joint of meat on
his table once in a quarter of a year.

Harvesters at Great Bedwin

(From *Rural Rides*, November 6, 1821.)

I LEFT Uphusband this morning at 9, and came across
to this place [Marlborough] in a post-chaise. Came up the
valley of Uphusband, which ends at about 6 miles from the
village, and puts one out upon the Wiltshire downs, which 10
stretch away towards the west and south-west, towards
Devizes and towards Salisbury. After about half a mile
of down we came down into a level country ; the flints
cease, and the chalk comes nearer the top of the ground.
The labourers along here seem very poor indeed. Farm
houses with twenty ricks round each, besides those standing
in the fields ; pieces of wheat, 50, 60, or 100 acres in a piece ;
but a group of women labourers, who were attending the
measurers to measure their reaping work, presented such
an assemblage of rags as I never before saw even amongst 20
the hoppers at Farnham, many of whom are common
beggars. I never before saw *country* people, and reapers
too, observe, so miserable in appearance as these. There
were some very pretty girls, but ragged as colts and as
pale as ashes. The day was cold too, and frost hardly off
the ground ; and their blue arms and lips would have
made any heart ache but that of a seatseller or a loan-
jobber. A little after passing by these poor things, whom
I left, cursing, as I went, those who had brought them to
this state, I came to a group of shabby houses upon a hill. 30
While a boy was watering his horses, I asked the ostler

the *name* of the place ; and, as the old women say, ' you might have knocked me down with a feather,' when he said, ' *Great Bedwin.*' The whole of the houses are not intrinsically worth a thousand pounds. There stood a thing out in the middle of the place, about 25 feet long and 15 wide, being a room stuck up on unhewed stone pillars about 10 feet high. It was the Town Hall, where the ceremony of choosing the *two members* is performed.

At Frome

(From *Rural Rides*, September 2, 1826.)

THIS appears to be a sort of little Manchester. A very small Manchester, indeed ; for it does not contain above ten to twelve thousand people, but it has all the *flash* of a Manchester, and the innkeepers and their people look and behave like the Manchester fellows. I was, I must confess, glad to find proofs of the irretrievable decay of the place. I remembered how ready the bluff manufacturers had been to *call in the troops* of various descriptions. ' Let them,' said I to myself, ' call the troops in now, to make their trade revive.'

English, Irish, and Scots

(From *Rural Rides*, June 19, 1822.)

FROM Kensington to this place [St. Albans], through Edgware, Stanmore, and Watford, the crop is almost entirely hay, from fields of permanent grass, manured by dung and other matter brought from the *Wen*. Near the Wen, where they have had the *first haul* of the Irish and other perambulating labourers, the hay is all in rick. Some miles further down it is nearly all in. Towards Stanmore and Watford, a third, perhaps, of the grass remains to be cut. It is curious to see how the thing regulates itself. We saw, all the way down, squads of

labourers, of different departments, migrating from tract
to tract ; leaving the cleared fields behind them and proceeding on towards the work to be yet performed ; and
then, as to the classes of labourers, the *mowers*, with their
scythes on their shoulders, were in front, going on towards
the standing crops, while the *hay-makers* were coming on
behind towards the grass already cut or cutting. The
weather is fair and warm ; so that the public-houses on
the road are pouring out their beer pretty fast, and are
getting a good share of the wages of these thirsty souls. 10
It is an exchange of beer for sweat ; but the tax-eaters
get, after all, the far greater part of the sweat ; for, if it
were not for the tax, the beer would sell for three-halfpence
a pot, instead of fivepence. Of this threepence-halfpenny
the Jews and jobbers get about twopence-halfpenny. It is
curious to observe how the different labours are divided as
to the *nations*. The mowers are all *English* ; the hay-
makers all *Irish*. Scotchmen toil hard enough in Scotland ;
but when they go from home it is not to *work*, if you please.
They are found in gardens, and especially in gentlemen's 20
gardens, tying up flowers, picking dead leaves off exotics,
peeping into melon-frames, publishing the banns of marriage between the ' *male* ' and ' *female* ' blossoms, tap-tap-
tapping against a wall with a hammer that weighs half an
ounce. They have backs as straight and shoulders as
square as heroes of Waterloo ; and who can blame them ?
The digging, the mowing, the carrying of loads ; all the
break-back and sweat-extracting work they leave to be
performed by those who have less *prudence* than they
have. The great purpose of human art, the great end of 30
human study, is to obtain *ease*, to throw the burden of
labour from our own shoulders and fix it on those of
others.

Better Fare on big Estates

(From *Rural Rides*, August 2, 1823.)

I SUPPOSE that every inch of land that I came through [from Petworth to Singleton] this morning belongs either to the Duke of Richmond or to Lord Egremont. No *harm* in that, mind, if those who till the land have *fair play* ; and I should act unjustly towards these noblemen, if I insinuated that the husbandmen have not fair play, as far as the land-lords are concerned ; for everybody speaks well of them. There is, besides, *no misery* to be seen here. I have seen no wretchedness in Sussex ; nothing to be at all compared
10 to that which I have seen in other parts ; and as to these villages in the South Downs, they are beautiful to behold. Hume and other historians rail against the *feudal*-system ; and we, ' enlightened ' and ' free ' creatures as we are, look back with scorn, or, at least, with surprise and pity, to the ' vassalage ' of our forefathers. But if the matter were well inquired into, not slurred over, but well and truly examined, we should find that the people of these villages were *as free* in the days of William Rufus as are the people of the present day ; and that vassalage, only under other
20 names, exists now as completely as it existed then. . . . There is an appearance of comfort about the dwellings of the labourers, all along here, that is very pleasant to behold. The gardens are neat, and full of vegetables of the best kinds. I see very few of ' Ireland's lazy root.'. . . As I came along between Upwaltham and Eastdean, I called to me a young man, who, along with other turnip-hoers, was sitting under the shelter of a hedge at breakfast. He came running to me with his victuals in his hand ; and I was glad to see that his food consisted of a good lump of
30 household bread and not a very small piece of *bacon*. I did not envy him his appetite, for I had at that moment a very good one of my own ; but I wanted to know the

distance I had to go before I should get to a good public-house. In parting with him, I said, ' You do get some *bacon* then ? '   ' Oh, yes ! sir,' said he, and with an emphasis and a swag of the head which seemed to say, ' We *must* and *will* have *that*.'   I saw, and with great delight, a pig at almost every labourer's house.   The houses are good and warm ; and the gardens some of the very best that I have seen in England.

Turnip-hoers at Avington

(From *Rural Rides*, August 6, 1823.)

THE turnips, upon this farm [at Avington] are by no means good ; but I was in some measure compensated for the bad turnips by the sight of the duke's turnip-hoers, about a dozen females, amongst whom there were several very pretty girls, and they were as merry as larks.   There had been a shower that had brought them into a sort of huddle on the roadside.   When I came up to them, they all fixed their eyes upon me, and upon my smiling, they bursted out into laughter.   I observed to them that the Duke of Buckingham was a very happy man to have such turnip-hoers, and really they seemed happier and better off than any work-people that I saw in the fields all the way from London to this spot.   It is curious enough, but I have always observed that the women along this part of the country are usually tall.   These girls were all tall, straight, fair, round-faced, excellent complexion, and uncommonly gay.   They were well dressed, too, and I observed the same of all the men that I saw down at Avington.   This could not be the case if the duke were a cruel or hard master ; and this is an act of justice due from me to the descendant of Rollo.

A favoured District

(From *Rural Rides*, November 14, 1821.)

RODE to the Forest of Dean, up a very steep hill. The lanes here are between high banks, and, on the sides of the hills, the road is a rock, the water having long ago washed all the earth away. Pretty works are, I find, carried on here, as is the case in all the other *public forests!* Are these things *always* to be carried on in this way? Here is a domain of thirty thousand acres of the finest timber-land in the world, and with coal-mines endless! Is this *worth nothing?* Cannot each acre yield ten trees a year? Are not these trees worth a pound a piece? Is not the estate worth three or four hundred thousand pounds a year? And does it yield *anything to the public*, to whom it belongs? But it is useless to waste one's breath in this way. We must have a *reform of the Parliament*: without it the whole thing will fall to pieces.—The only good purpose that these forests answer is that of furnishing a place of being to labourers' families on their skirts; and here their cottages are very neat, and the people look hearty and well, just as they do round the forests in Hampshire. Every cottage has a pig, or two. These graze in the forest, and, in the fall, eat acorns and beech-nuts and the seed of the ash; for, these last, as well as the others, are very full of oil, and a pig that is put to his shifts will pick the seed very nicely out from the husks. Some of these foresters keep cows, and all of them have bits of ground, cribbed, of course, at different times, from the forest: and to what better use can the ground be put? I saw several wheat stubbles from 40 rods to 10 rods. I asked one man how much wheat he had from about 10 rods. He said more than two bushels. Here is bread for three weeks, or more, perhaps; and a winter's straw for the pig beside. Are these things nothing? The dead limbs and old roots of the forest give *fuel* ; and how happy are these people, compared with the poor creatures about Great Bedwin and Cricklade, where they have neither land nor shelter, and where I saw the girls carrying home bean and wheat stubble for fuel ! Those countries, always but badly furnished with fuel, the desolating and damnable system of paper-money, by sweeping away small homesteads, and laying ten farms into one, has literally *stripped* of all shelter for the labourer.

The old Farmhouse and the new

(From *Rural Rides*, October 20, 1825.)

REIGATE,   10

Wednesday Evening, 19 *October,* 1825.

HAVING some business at Hartswood, near Reigate, I intended to come off this morning on horseback, along with my son Richard, but it rained so furiously the last night that we gave up the horse project for to-day, being, by appointment, to be at Reigate by ten o'clock to-day: so that we came off this morning at five o'clock in a post-chaise, intending to return home and take our horses. Finding, however, that we cannot quit this place till Friday, we have now sent for our horses, though the 20 weather is dreadfully wet. But we are under a farm-house roof, and the wind may whistle and the rain fall as much as they like.

REIGATE,

Thursday Evening, 20 *October.*

Having done my business at Hartswood to-day about eleven o'clock, I went to a sale at a farm, which the farmer is quitting. Here I had a view of what has long been going on all over the country. The farm, which belongs to *Christ's Hospital,* has been held by a man of the name of 30 Charington, in whose family the lease has been, I hear, a great number of years. The house is hidden by trees. It stands in the Weald of Surrey, close by the *River Mole*, which is here a mere rivulet, though just below this house the rivulet supplies the very prettiest flour-mill I ever saw in my life.

Everything about this farm-house was formerly the scene of *plain manners* and *plentiful living*. Oak clothes-chests, oak bedsteads, oak chests of drawers, and oak tables to eat on, long, strong, and well supplied with joint stools.
10 Some of the things were many hundreds of years old. But all appeared to be in a state of decay and nearly of *disuse*. There appeared to have been hardly any *family* in that house, where formerly there were, in all probability, from ten to fifteen men, boys, and maids : and, which was the worst of all, there was a *parlour*. Aye, and a *carpet* and *bell-pull* too ! One end of the front of this once plain and substantial house had been moulded into a ' *parlour* ;' and there was the mahogany table, and the fine chairs, and the fine glass, and all as bare-faced upstart as any stock-
20 jobber in the kingdom can boast of. And there were the decanters, the glasses, the ' dinner-set ' of crockery-ware, and all just in the true stock-jobber style. And I dare say it has been '*Squire* Charington and the *Miss* Charingtons ; and not plain Master Charington, and his son Hodge, and his daughter Betty Charington, all of whom this accursed system has, in all likelihood, transmuted into a species of mock gentlefolks, while it has ground the labourers down into real slaves. . . . The land produces, on an average, what it always produced, but there is a new distribution of the
30 produce. This '*Squire* Charington's father used, I dare say, to sit at the head of the oak table along with his men, say grace to them, and cut up the meat and the pudding. He might take a cup of *strong beer* to himself, when they had none ; but that was pretty nearly all the difference in their manner of living. So that *all* lived well. But the '*squire*

had many *wine-decanters* and *wine-glasses* and ' *a dinner set*,' and a ' *breakfast set*,' and ' *dessert knives* ; ' and these evidently imply carryings on and a consumption that must of necessity have greatly robbed the long oak table if it had remained fully tenanted. . . .

I could not quit this farm-house without reflecting on the thousands of scores of bacon and thousands of bushels of bread that had been eaten from the long oak-table which, I said to myself, is now perhaps going at last to the bottom of a bridge that some stock-jobber will stick up 10 over an artificial river in his cockney garden. ' *By* —— *it shan't*,' said I, almost in a real passion : and so I requested a friend to buy it for me ; and if he do so, I will take it to Kensington, or to Fleet Street, and keep it for the good it has done in the world.

The Loss of Cottage Industries

(From *Rural Rides*, August 1, 1823.)

TO-DAY, near a place called Westborough Green, I saw a woman bleaching her home-spun and home-woven linen. I have not seen such a thing before, since I left Long Island. There, and, indeed, all over the American States, north of Maryland, and especially in the New England States, almost 20 the whole of both linen and woollen, used in the country, and a large part of that used in towns, is made in the farm-houses.   There are thousands and thousands of families who never use either, except of their own making. All but the weaving is done by the family.   There is a loom in the house, and the weaver goes from house to house. I once saw about three thousand farmers, or rather country people, at a horse race in Long Island, and my opinion was, that there were not five hundred who were not dressed in home-spun coats.   As to linen, no farmer's family thinks 30 of buying linen.   The lords of the loom have taken from

the land, in England, this part of its due ; and hence one
cause of the poverty, misery, and pauperism that are
becoming so frightful throughout the country. A national
debt, and all the taxation and gambling belonging to it,
have a natural tendency to draw wealth into great masses.
These masses produce a power of *congregating* manu-
factures, and of making the many work at them, for the
gain of a few. The taxing government finds great convenience in these congregations. It can lay its hand easily
10 upon a part of the produce ; as ours does with so much
effect. But the land suffers greatly from this, and the
country must finally feel the fatal effects of it. The country
people lose part of their natural employment. The women
and children, who ought to provide a great part of the
raiment, have nothing to do. The fields *must* have men
and boys ; but where there are men and boys there will
be *women* and *girls* ; and as the lords of the loom have now
a set of real slaves, by the means of whom they take away
a great part of the employment of the country-women and
20 girls, these must be kept by poor rates in whatever degree
they lose employment through the lords of the loom. One
would think that nothing can be much plainer than this ;
and yet you hear the *jolterheads* congratulating one another
upon the increase of Manchester, and such places !

The Curse of Locomotion

(From *Rural Rides*, August 24, 1826.)

I GOT, at one time, a little out of my road in or near
a place called Tangley. I rode up to the garden wicket of
a cottage, and asked the woman, who had two children,
and who seemed to be about thirty years old, which was
the way to Ludgershall, which I knew could not be more
30 than about *four miles* off. She did *not know !* A very neat,
smart, and pretty woman ; but she did not know the way

to this rotten borough, which was, I was sure, only about four miles off ! ' Well, my dear good woman,' said I, ' but you *have been* at Ludgershall ? '—' No.'—' Nor at Andover ? ' (six miles another way)—' No.'—' Nor at Marlborough ? ' (nine miles another way)—' No.'—' Pray, were you born in this house ? '—' Yes.'—' And how far have you ever been from this house ? '—' Oh ! I have been *up in the parish* and over *to Chute.*' That is to say, the utmost extent of her voyages had been about two and a half miles ! Let no one laugh at her, and, above all others, let not me, who am convinced that the *facilities* which now exist of *moving human bodies from place to place* are amongst the *curses* of the country, the destroyers of industry, of morals, and, of course, of happiness. It is a great error to suppose that people are rendered stupid by remaining always in the same place. This was a very acute woman, and as well behaved as need to be.

The Drain of London

(From *Rural Rides*, October 2, 1826.)

WE had to come through Swindon, and Mr. Tucky had the kindness to come with us, until we got three or four miles on this side (the Hungerford side) of that very neat and plain and solid and respectable market town. Swindon is in Wiltshire, and is in the real fat of the land, all being wheat, beans, cheese, or fat meat. In our way to Swindon, Mr. Tucky's farm exhibited to me what I never saw before, four score oxen, all grazing upon one farm, and all nearly fat ! They were some Devonshire and some Herefordshire. They were fatting on the grass only, and I should suppose that they are worth, or shortly will be, thirty pounds each. But the great pleasure with which the contemplation of this fine sight was naturally calculated to inspire me was more than counterbalanced by the thought that these fine oxen, this primest of human food, was, aye, every mouthful of it, destined to be devoured in the Wen, and that too, for the far greater part, by the Jews, loan-jobbers, tax-eaters, and their base and prostituted followers . . . literary as well as other wretches, who, if suffered to live at all, ought to partake of nothing but the offal, and ought to come but one cut before the dogs and cats !

Decline of Markets and Fairs

(From *Rural Rides*, October 22, 1826.)

A VILLAGE it [Hambledon] *now* is ; but it was formerly a considerable market-town, and it had three fairs in the
10 year. There is now not even the name of market left, I believe ; and the fairs amount to little more than a couple or three gingerbread-stalls, with dolls and whistles for children. If you go through the place, you see that it has been a considerable town. The church tells the same story ; it is now a tumble-down rubbishy place ; it is partaking in the fate of all those places which were formerly a sort of rendezvous for persons who had things to buy and things to sell. *Wens* have devoured market-towns and villages ; and *shops* have devoured *markets and fairs* ; and
20 this, too, to the infinite injury of the most numerous classes of the people. Shop-keeping, merely as shop-keeping, is injurious to any community. . . .

When fairs were very frequent shops were not needed. A manufacturer of shoes, of stockings, of hats ; of almost anything that man wants, could manufacture at home in an obscure hamlet, with cheap house-rent, good air, and plenty of room. He need pay no heavy rent for shop ; and no disadvantages from confined situation ; and then, by attending three or four or five or six fairs a year, he
30 sold the work of his hands, unloaded with a heavy expense attending the keeping of a shop. He would get more for

ten shillings in a booth at a fair or market than he would
get in a shop for ten or twenty pounds. Of course he could
afford to sell the work of his hands for less ; and thus
a greater portion of their earnings remained with those
who raised the food and the clothing from the land. . . .
Does not every one see, in a minute, how this exchanging
of fairs and markets for shops creates *idlers and traffickers ;*
creates those locusts called middlemen who create nothing,
who add to the value of nothing, who improve nothing,
but who live in idleness, and who live well, too, out of the 10
labour of the producer and the consumer.

Decline of the Gentry

(From *Rural Rides*, October 31, 1825.)

Not so the product of the little sedgy rivulet of Whitchurch ! It has, in the short space of a hundred and thirty-
one years, and, indeed, in the space of the last *forty*, caused
greater changes as to property than had been caused by
all other things put together in the long course of seven
centuries, though during that course there had been a sweeping, confiscating Protestant reformation. Let us look back
to the place where I started on this present rural ride.
Poor old Baron Maseres succeeded at Reigate by little 20
Parson Fellowes, and at Betchworth (three miles on my
road) by Kendrick, is no bad instance to begin with ; for
the Baron was nobly descended, though from French
ancestors. At Albury, fifteen miles on my road, Mr. Drummond (a banker) is in the seat of one of the Howards, and,
close by, he has bought the estate, just pulled down the
house, and blotted out the memory of the Godschalls.
At Chilworth, two miles further down the same vale, and
close under St. Martha's Hill, Mr. Tinkler, a powder-maker
(succeeding Hill, another powder-maker, who had been 30
a breeches-maker at Hounslow) has got the old mansion

and the estate of the old Duchess of Marlborough, who
frequently resided in what was then a large quadrangular
mansion, but the remains of which now serve as out farm-
buildings and a farm-house, which I found inhabited by
a poor labourer and his family, the farm being in the hands
of the powder-maker, who does not find the once noble
seat good enough for him. Coming on to Waverley Abbey,
there is Mr. Thompson, a merchant, succeeding the Orby
Hunters and Sir Robert Rich. Close adjoining, Mr. Laing,
10 a West India dealer of some sort, has stepped into the place
of the lineal descendants of Sir William Temple. At Farnham the park and palace remain in the hands of a Bishop
of Winchester, as they have done for about eight hundred
years : but why is this ? Because they are public property ;
because they cannot, without express laws, be transferred.
Therefore the product of the rivulet of Whitchurch has
had no effect upon the ownership of these, which are still
in the hands of a Bishop of Winchester ; not of a William
of Wykham, to be sure ; but still in those of a bishop, at
20 any rate. Coming on to old Alresford (twenty miles from
Farnham) Sheriff, the son of a Sheriff, who was a com-
missary in the American war, has succeeded the Gages.
Two miles further on, at Abbotston (down on the side of
the Itchen) Alexander Baring has succeeded the heirs and
successors of the Duke of Bolton, the remains of whose
noble mansion I once saw here. Not above a mile higher
up, the same Baring has, at the Grange, with its noble
mansion, park and estate, succeeded the heirs of Lord
Northington ; and at only about two miles further, Sir
30 Thomas Baring, at Stratton Park, has succeeded the
Russells in the ownership of the estates of Stratton and
Micheldover, which were once the property of Alfred the
Great ! Stepping back, and following my road, down by
the side of the meadows of the beautiful river Itchen, and
coming to Easton, I look across to Martyr's Worthy, and

there see (as I observed before) the Ogles succeeded by a general or a colonel somebody; but who, or whence, I cannot learn.

This is all in less than four score miles, from Reigate even to this place where I now am. Oh! mighty rivulet of Whitchurch! All our properties, all our laws, all our manners, all our minds, you have changed! This, which I have noticed, has all taken place within forty, and, most of it, within *ten* years. The *small gentry*, to about the *third* rank upwards (considering there to be five ranks from 10 the smallest gentry up to the greatest nobility), are *all gone*, nearly to a man, and the small farmers along with them. The Barings alone have, I should think, swallowed up thirty or forty of these small gentry without perceiving it. They, indeed, swallow up the biggest race of all; but innumerable small fry slip down unperceived, like caplins down the throats of the sharks, while these latter *feel* only the cod-fish. It frequently happens, too, that a big gentleman or nobleman, whose estate has been big enough to resist for a long while, and who has swilled up many caplin- 20 gentry, goes down the throat of the loan-dealer with all the caplins in his belly.

(From *A Legacy to Peel*, 1836. Sir James Graham having written a pamphlet to propose deducting 30 per cent. from the interest on the Debt, Cobbett declared in *The Register* that the people would first demand a reduction of sinecures and pensions. The following is a conversation supposed to take place at a country house :)

LORD HUMDRUM. I have been thinking, my dear, about this pamphlet of Graham; and I begin to think that it would not do.

LADY HUMDRUM. How changeable you are, my dear. Why, it was but yesterday that you said it would save us all, and pay off the mortgage of that vile wretch Mordecai, who really comes into the house as if he were the master of us all; and the beast the other day had the impudence to 30

bow and to compliment Isabella, observing that he would
be a happy man who should lead her to the altar.

LORD H. Well, my dear, . . . we have got his money
and can't pay him off.

LADY H. But you said that Graham's project would
pay him off all at once ; and now you have changed your
mind without any reason.

LORD H. No, my love, not without reason.

LADY H. Well, what reason have you then ?

10   LORD H. Why, to tell you the truth, I yesterday at Sir
John Jolterhead's saw a publication in answer to Graham.
. . . It's a little publication that is put up at London ; and
though I never saw it before, and though I detest the
author, I . . .

LADY H. Well, but what publication is it ?

LORD H. I don't like to tell you, my love, because I
am afraid it will throw you into a passion. Well, then, I
was over at Sir John's yesterday ; he wasn't at home ;
but I found Mr. Sharpshins, the steward, waiting for him.
20 He was reading a paper, and, seeing me, he crammed it
into his pocket. I insisted upon seeing it, and when he
pulled it out, I found that it was Cobb . . .

LADY H. (*falling on a sofa*). Oh, wretched man ! and
have you been reading the trash of that bloody-minded
villain, who has so often instigated the people to chop us
all up, and fling us to the hogs ?

LORD H. Well, my love, . . . you know how I have been
trying to get something against him to cause him to be
hanged ; but you know that, as the poet says, ' we may
30 profit from the reasonings of our enemies '.

LADY H. Don't tell me of profiting by reading Cobbett,
that monster, whom neither jails nor banishment can kill.

LORD H. Whether the fellow wrote the paper or not I
don't know : but it has convinced me we shall be ruined by
the adoption of the project of Graham . . .

LADY H. Can't you send and borrow it from Mr. Sharpshins ?

LORD H. I don't know that Mr. Sharpshins would like to have it known that he takes it in.

LADY H. Can't you send and get it from London ? I want to see it so monstrously.

LORD H. (*slipping his hand into his coat-pocket, pulling out the Register, and tossing it down upon the table*). There it is, then, my dear.

LADY H. (*Starting back.*) Oh, Lord ! I almost think I see the devil !

LORD H. Well, now, do be cool a little, and I will read the paper to you all through. (*He reads*) . . .

LADY H. (*When my Lord comes to the word ' sinecure '*) Oh, Lord ! (*After hearing contents of paper*) Well, how can we lose by the adoption of Sir James Graham's proposition ?

LORD H. Take that piece of paper, my dear, and the pen, and we will see now.

Loss	£
Money paid to fundholder in taxes	2,000

Gain	£
Amount of sinecure to myself, deducting tax	700
Amount of my half-pay as a General	500
Amount of Tom's pay as a Captain, clear of expenses	100
Amount of Harriet's husband's half-pay, as Lieutenant-Colonel	400
Amount of David's full pay and bat and coal and candle money	400
Amount of the living of Sarah's husband in the parish of Tumble-Church, a clear	700

	£
Value of the seven yearly weedings of the forest, per annum	1,300
Dick's salary as Commissioner of Excise . .	1,000
Peter's income as Distributor of Stamps . .	800
	5,900
	2,000
	£3,900

LORD H. Thus, you see, my dear, we should lose £3,900 a year by clever Graham's invention to save our estates.

10   LADY H. What a fool that Graham must be not to see this ! And this villain, Cobbett, is our best friend after all.

Decline of Rural Population
(From *Rural Rides*, August 31, 1826.)

FROM Heytesbury to Warminster is a part of the country singularly bright and beautiful. From Salisbury up to very near Heytesbury you have the valley as before described by me. Meadows next the water ; then arable land ; then the downs ; but when you come to Heytesbury, and indeed, a little before, in looking forward you see the vale stretch out, from about three miles wide to ten miles wide, from high land to high land. From a hill before you come down 20 to Heytesbury you see through this wide opening into Somersetshire. You see a round hill rising in the middle of the opening ; but all the rest a flat enclosed country, and apparently full of wood. In looking back down this vale one cannot help being struck with the innumerable proofs that there are of a decline in point of population. In the first place, there are twenty-four parishes, each of which takes a little strip across the valley, and runs up through the arable land into the down. There are twenty-four parish churches, and there ought to be as many 30 *parsonage-houses* ; but seven of these, out of the twenty-

four, that is to say, nearly one-third of them, are, in the
returns laid before parliament (and of which returns I shall
speak more particularly by and by), stated to be such
miserable dwellings as to be unfit for a parson to reside in.
Two of them, however, are gone. There are no parsonage-
houses in those two parishes : there are the sites ; there
are the glebes ; but the houses have been suffered to
fall down and to be totally carried away. The tithes
remain, indeed, and the parson sacks the amount of them.
A journeyman parson comes and works in three or four 10
churches of a Sunday ; but the master parson is not there.
He generally carries away the produce to spend it in
London, at Bath, or somewhere else, to show off his
daughters ; and the overseers, that is to say, the farmers,
manage the poor in their own way, instead of having,
according to the ancient law, a third-part of all the tithes
to keep them with.

The falling down and the beggary of these parsonage-
houses prove beyond all question the decayed state of the
population. And, indeed, the mansion-houses are gone, 20
except in a very few instances. There are but five left
that I could perceive, all the way from Salisbury to
Warminster, though the country is the most pleasant
that can be imagined. Here is water, here are meadows ;
plenty of fresh-water fish ; hares and partridges in abundance, and it is next to impossible to destroy them. Here
are shooting, coursing, hunting ; hills of every height, size,
and form ; valleys the same ; lofty trees and rookeries in
every mile ; roads always solid and good ; always pleasant
for exercise ; and the air must be of the best in the world. 30
Yet it is manifest that four-fifths of the mansions have
been swept away. There is a parliamentary return to
prove that nearly a third of the parsonage-houses have
become beggarly holes or have disappeared. I have now
been in nearly three score villages, and in twenty or thirty

or forty hamlets of Wiltshire ; and I do not know that
I have been in one, however small, in which I did not see
a house or two, and sometimes more, either tumbled down
or beginning to tumble down. It is impossible for the eyes
of man to be fixed on a finer country than that between
the village of Codford and the town of Warminster ; and
it is not very easy for the eyes of man to discover labouring
people more miserable. There are two villages, one called
Norton Bovant and the other Bishopstrow, which I think
10 form together one of the prettiest spots that my eyes ever
beheld. The former village belongs to Bennet, the member
for the county, who has a mansion there, in which two of
his sisters live, I am told. There is a farm at Bishopstrow,
standing at the back of the arable land, up in a vale
formed by two very lofty hills, upon each of which there
was formerly a Roman camp, in consideration of which
farm, if the owner would give it me, I would almost consent
to let Ottiwell Wood remain quiet in his seat, and suffer
the pretty gentlemen of Whitehall to go on without note
20 or comment till they had fairly blowed up their concern.
The farm-yard is surrounded by lofty and beautiful trees.
In the rick-yard I counted twenty-two ricks of one sort
and another. The hills shelter the house and the yard
and the trees most completely from every wind but the
south. The arable land goes down before the house, and
spreads along the edge of the down, going with a gentle
slope down to the meadows. So that, going along the
turnpike-road, which runs between the lower fields of the
arable land, you see the large and beautiful flocks of sheep
30 upon the sides of the down, while the horn-cattle are up
to their eyes in grass in the meadows. Just when I was
coming along here, the sun was about half an hour high ;
it shined through the trees most brilliantly ; and, to crown
the whole, I met, just as I was entering the village, a very
pretty girl, who was apparently going a gleaning in the

fields. I asked her the name of the place, and when she told me it was Bishopstrow, she pointed to the situation of the church, which, she said, was on the other side of the river. She really put me in mind of the pretty girls at Preston who spat upon the 'individual' of the Derby family, and I made her a bow accordingly.

The whole of the population of the twenty-four parishes down this vale amounts to only 11,195 souls, according to the official return to parliament; and, mind, I include the parish of Fisherton Anger (a suburb of the city of Salisbury), which contains 893 of the number. I include the town of Heytesbury, with its 1023 souls; and I further include this very good and large market town of Warminster, with its population of 5000! So that I leave, in the other twenty-one parishes, only 4170 souls, men, women, and children! That is to say, a hundred and ninety-eight souls to each parish; or, reckoning five to a family, thirty-nine families to each parish. Above one half of the population never could be expected to be in the church at one time; so that here are one-and-twenty churches built for the purpose of holding 2080 people! There are several of these churches, any one of which would conveniently contain the whole of these people, the 2080! The church of Bishopstrow would contain the whole of the 2080 very well indeed; and it is curious enough to observe that the churches of Fisherton Anger, Heytesbury, and Warminster, though quite sufficient to contain the people that go to church, are none of them nearly so big as several of the village churches. All these churches are built long and long before the reign of Richard II.; that is to say, they were founded long before that time, and if the first churches were gone, these others were built in their stead. There is hardly one of them that is not as old as the reign of Richard II.; and yet that impudent Scotchman, George Chalmers, would make us believe that, in the reign of Richard II., the population of the country was hardly anything at all ! He has the impudence, or the gross ignorance, to state the population of England and Wales at *two millions*, which, as I have shown in the last number of the Protestant Reformation, would allow only twelve able men to every parish church throughout the kingdom. What, I ask, for about the thousandth time I ask it, what were these twenty churches built for ? Some of them stand within a quarter of a mile of each other. They are pretty nearly as close to each other as the churches in London and Westminster are.

What a monstrous thing to suppose that they were built without there being people to go to them ; and built, too, without money and without hands ! The whole of the population in these twenty-one parishes could stand, and without much crowding too, in the bottoms of the towers of the several churches. Nay, in three or four of the parishes, the whole of the people could stand in the church porches. Then the *church-yards* show you how numerous the population must have been. You see, in some cases, only here and there the mark of a grave, where the church-yard contains from half an acre to an acre of land, and sometimes more. In short, everything shows that here was once a great and opulent population ; that there was an abundance to eat, to wear, and to spare ; that all the land that is now under cultivation, and a great deal that is not now under cultivation, was under cultivation in former times.

Indifference to Parliament

(From *Rural Rides*, October 31, 1825.)

THERE is, in fact, *no opposition ;* and this is felt by the whole nation ; and this is the reason why *the people* now take so little interest in what is said and done in parliament, compared to that which they formerly took. This is the reason why there is no man, or men, whom the people seem to care at all about. A great portion of the people now clearly understand the nature and effects of the system ; they are not now to be deceived by speeches and professions. If Pitt and Fox had *now to start*, there would be no ' Pittites ' and ' Foxites.' Those happy days of political humbug are gone for ever. The ' gentlemen *opposite* ' are opposite only as to mere *local position.* They sit on the opposite side of the house : that's all. In every other respect they are like parson and clerk ; or, 10 perhaps, rather more like the rooks and jackdaws : one *caw* and the other *chatter* ; but both have the same object in view : both are in pursuit of the same sort of diet. One set is, to be sure, IN place, and the other OUT ; but though the rooks keep the jackdaws on the inferior branches these latter would be as clamorous as the rooks themselves against *felling the tree !*

Moral Degeneracy

(From the *Advice to Young Men.*)

ONE great source of the unhappiness amongst mankind arises, however, from a neglect of these duties ; but, as if by way of compensation for their privations, they are 20 much more duly performed by the poor than by the rich. The fashion of the labouring people is this : the husband, when free from his toil in the fields, takes his share in the nursing, which he manifestly looks upon as a sort of reward for his labour. However distant from his cottage, his heart is always at that home towards which he is carried, at night, by limbs that feel not their weariness, being urged on by a heart anticipating the welcome of those who attend him there. Those who have, as I so many hundreds of times have, seen the labourers in the woodland 30 parts of Hampshire and Sussex, coming, at night-fall, towards their cottage-wickets, laden with fuel for a day or

two ; whoever has seen three or four little creatures looking out for the father's approach, running in to announce the glad tidings, and then scampering out to meet him, clinging round his knees, or hanging on his skirts ; whoever has witnessed scenes like this, to witness which has formed one of the greatest delights of my life, will hesitate long before he prefer a life of ease to a life of labour ; before he prefer a communication with children intercepted by servants and teachers to that communication which is here direct, and
10 which admits not of any division of affection.

Then comes *the Sunday ;* and, amongst all those who keep no servants, a great deal depends on the manner in which the father employs *that day.* When there are two or three children, or even one child, the first thing, after the breakfast (which is late on this day of rest), is to wash and dress the child or children. Then, while the mother is dressing the dinner, the father, being in his Sunday clothes himself, takes care of the child or children. When dinner is over, the mother puts on her best ; and then, all go to
20 church, or, if that cannot be, whether from distance or other cause, *all pass the afternoon together.* This used to be the way of life amongst the labouring people ; and from this way of life arose the most able and most moral people that the world ever saw, until grinding taxation took from them the means of obtaining a sufficiency of food and of raiment ; plunged the whole, good and bad, into one indiscriminate mass, under the degrading and hateful name of paupers.

The Odds against the Poor
(From *Rural Rides,* October 31, 1825.)

BEFORE we got this supply of bread and cheese, we,
30 though in ordinary times a couple of singularly jovial companions, and seldom going a hundred yards (except going very fast) without one or the other speaking,

began to grow *dull*, or rather *glum*.   The way seemed
long ; and, when I had to speak in answer to Richard,
the speaking was as brief as might be.   Unfortunately,
just at this critical period, one of the loops that held
the straps of Richard's little portmanteau broke ; and it
became necessary (just before we overtook Mr. Bailey) for
me to fasten the portmanteau on before me, upon my
saddle.   This, which was not the work of more than five
minutes, would, had I had *a breakfast*, have been nothing
at all, and, indeed, matter of laughter.   But, *now*, it was 10
something.   It was his '*fault*' for capering and jerking
about ' *so*.'   I jumped off, saying, ' *Here !* I'll carry it
myself.'   And then I began to take off the remaining strap,
pulling with great violence and in great haste.   Just at
this time my eyes met his, in which I saw *great surprise ;*
and, feeling the just rebuke, feeling heartily ashamed of
myself, I instantly changed my tone and manner, cast the
blame upon the saddler, and talked of the effectual means
which we would take to prevent the like in future.

Now, if such was the effect produced upon me by the 20
want of food for only two or three hours ; me, who had
dined well the day before and eaten toast and butter the
over night ; if the missing of only one breakfast, and that,
too, from my own whim, while I had money in my pocket,
to get one at any public-house, and while I could get one
only for asking for at any farm-house ; if the not having
breakfasted could, and under such circumstances, make me
what you may call ' *cross* ' to a child like this, whom I must
necessarily love so much, and to whom I never speak but
in the very kindest manner ;   if this mere absence of 30
a breakfast could thus put me *out of temper*, how great are
the allowances that we ought to make for the poor creatures
who, in this once happy and now miserable country, are
doomed to lead a life of constant labour and of half
starvation.

A CHAPTER OF JUDGEMENTS

Food and Morals

(From *Cottage Economy*.)

I LAY it down as a maxim, that, for a family to be
happy, they must be well supplied with *food* and *raiment*.
It is a sorry effort that people make to persuade others, or
to persuade themselves, that they can be happy in a state
of *want* of the necessaries of life. The doctrines, which
fanaticism preaches, and which teach men to be *content*
with *poverty*, have a very pernicious tendency, and are
calculated to favour tyrants by giving them passive slaves.
To live well, to enjoy all things that make life pleasant, is
10 the right of every man who constantly uses his strength
judiciously and lawfully. It is to blaspheme God to suppose,
that he created men to be miserable, to hunger, thirst,
and perish with cold, in the midst of that abundance which
is the fruit of their own labour. Instead, therefore, of
applauding ' *happy* poverty ', which applause is so much
the fashion of the present day, I despise the man that is
poor and *contented ;* for, such content is a certain proof of
a base disposition, a disposition which is the enemy of all
industry, all exertion, all love of independence.

20 Let it be understood, however, that, by *poverty*, I mean
real want, a real insufficiency of the food and raiment and
lodging necessary to health and decency ; and not that
imaginary poverty, of which some persons complain. The
man who, by his own and his family's labour, can provide
a sufficiency of food and raiment and a comfortable dwelling
place, is not a *poor man*. There must be different ranks and
degrees in every civil society, and, indeed, so it is even
amongst the savage tribes. There must be different degrees

of wealth ; some must have more than others ; and the
richest must be a great deal richer than the least rich. But
it is necessary to the very existence of a people, that nine
out of ten should live wholly by the sweat of their brow ;
and, is it not degrading to human nature, that all the nine
tenths should be called *poor ;* and, what is still worse, *call
themselves poor*, and be *contented* in that degraded state ?

The laws, the economy, or management, of a state
may be such as to render it impossible for the labourer,
however skilful and industrious, to maintain his family in 10
health and decency ; and such has, for many years past,
been the management of the affairs of this once truly great
and happy land. A system of paper-money, the effect of
which was to take from the labourer the half of his earnings,
was what no industry and care could make head against.
I do not pretend, that this system was adopted *by design*.
But, no matter for the *cause ;* such was the effect.

Better times, however, are approaching. The labourer
now appears likely to obtain that hire of which he is worthy ;
and therefore, this appears to me to be the time to press 20
upon him the *duty* of using his best exertions for the rearing
of his family in a manner that must give him the best security
for happiness to himself, his wife and children, and to make
him, in all respects, what his forefathers were. The people
of England have been famed, in all ages, for their *good
living ;* for the *abundance of their food* and *goodness of
their attire*. The old sayings about English roast beef and
plumb-pudding, and about English hospitality, had not their
foundation in *nothing*. And, in spite of all the refinements
of sickly minds, it is *abundant living* amongst the people at 30
large, which is the great test of good government, and the
surest basis of national greatness and security.

In Praise of the Goat

(From *Cottage Economy*.)

IN some places, where a cow cannot be kept, a Goat may.
A correspondent points out to me, that a Dorset ewe or two
might be kept on a common near a cottage to give milk ;
and certainly this might be done very well ; but, I should
prefer a goat, which is hardier, and much more domestic.
When I was in the army, in New Brunswick, where, be it
observed, the snow lies on the ground seven months in the
year, there were many goats that *belonged to the regiment,*
and that went about with it on shipboard and every where
else. Some of them had gone through nearly the whole of
the *American War.* We *never fed* them. In summer they
picked about wherever they could find grass ; and in winter
they lived on cabbage-leaves, turnip-peelings, potatoe-
peelings, and other things flung out of the soldiers' rooms
and huts. One of these goats belonged to me, and, on an
average throughout the year, she gave me more than three
half pints of milk a day. I used to have the kid killed
when a few days old ; and, for some time, the goat would
give nearly, or quite, two quarts of milk a day. She was
seldom dry more than three weeks in the year.

There is one great inconvenience belonging to goats ;
that is, they bark all young trees that they come near ; so
that, if they get into a *garden,* they destroy every thing.
But, there are seldom trees on commons, except such as are
too large to be injured by goats ; and I can see no reason
against keeping a goat, where a cow cannot be kept. Nothing
is so hardy ; nothing so little nice as to its food. Goats
will pick peelings out of the kennel and eat them. They
will eat mouldy bread or biscuit ; fusty hay, and almost
rotten straw ; furze-bushes, heath, thistles ; and, indeed,
what will they not eat, when they will make a hearty meal
on *paper*, brown or white, printed on or not printed on, and

give milk all the while. They will lie in any dog-hole. They do very well clogged, or stumped out. And, then, they are very *healthy* things into the bargain, however closely they may be confined. When sea voyages are so stormy as to kill geese, ducks, fowls, and almost pigs, the goats are well and lively ; and when a dog of no kind can keep the deck for a minute, a goat will skip about upon it as bold as brass.

Goats do not *ramble* from home. They come in regularly in the evening, and, if called, they come, like dogs. Now, though Ewes, when taken great care of, will be very gentle, and though their milk may be rather more delicate than that of the goat, the Ewes must be fed with nice and clean food, and they will not do much in the milk-giving way upon a common ; and, as to *feeding them,* provision must be made pretty nearly as for a cow. They will not endure *confinement* like goats ; and they are subject to numerous ailments that goats know nothing of. Then the Ewes are done by the time they are about six years old ; for they then lose their teeth ; whereas a goat will continue to breed and to give milk in abundance for a great many years. The sheep is *frightened* at every thing, and especially at the least sound of a dog. A goat, on the contrary, will *face a dog*, and if he be not a big and courageous one, beat him off.

I have often wondered how it happened that none of our labourers kept goats ; and I really should be glad to see the thing tried. They are pretty creatures, domestic as a dog, will stand and watch, as a dog does, for a crumb of bread, as you are eating ; give you no trouble in the milking ; and I cannot help being of opinion, that it might be of great use to introduce them amongst our labourers.

Tea

(From *Cottage Economy*.)

THE drink, which has come to supply the place of beer has, in general, been *tea*. It is notorious, that tea has no *useful strength* in it ; that it contains nothing *nutricious* ; that it, besides being *good* for nothing, has *badness* in it, because it is well known to produce want of sleep in many cases, and in all cases to shake and weaken the nerves. It is, in fact, a weaker kind of laudanum, which enlivens for the moment and deadens afterwards. At any rate it communicates no strength to the body ; it does not, in any 10 degree, assist in affording what labour demands. It is, then, of no *use*. And, now, as to its *cost*, compared with that of *beer*. I shall make my comparison applicable to a year, or three hundred and sixty-five days. I shall suppose the tea to be only five shillings the pound ; the sugar only sevenpence ; the milk only twopence a quart. The prices are at the very lowest. I shall suppose a tea-pot to cost a shilling, six cups and saucers two shillings and sixpence, and six pewter spoons eighteen pence. How to estimate the firing I hardly know ; but certainly there must, in the course of 20 the year, be two hundred fires made that would not be made, were it not for tea drinking. Then comes the great article of all, the *time* employed in this tea making affair. It is impossible to make a fire, boil water, make the tea, drink it, wash up the things, sweep up the fire-place and put all to rights again in a less space of time, upon an average, than *two hours*. However, let us allow *one hour* ; and here we have a woman occupied no less than three hundred and sixty-five hours in the year, or, thirty whole days, at twelve hours in the day ; that is to say, one month out of the 30 twelve in the year, besides the waste of the man's time in hanging about waiting for the tea ! Needs there any thing more to make us cease to wonder at seeing labourers' children with dirty linen and holes in the heels of their stockings ?

The First Principle of Education

(From the *Advice to Young Men.*)

THE great matter is, however, the *spoiling of the mind* by forcing on it thoughts which it is not fit to receive. We know well, we daily see, that in men, as well as in other animals, the body is rendered comparatively small and feeble by being heavily loaded, or hard worked, before it arrive at size and strength proportioned to such load and such work. It is just so with the mind : the attempt to put 10 old heads upon young shoulders is just as unreasonable as it would be to expect a colt six months old to be able to carry a man. The mind, as well as the body, requires time to come to its strength ; and the way to have it possess, at last, its natural strength, is not to attempt to load it too soon; and to favour it in its progress by giving to the body good and plentiful food, sweet air, and abundant exercise, accompanied with as little discontent or uneasiness as possible. It is universally known that ailments of the body are, in many cases, sufficient to *destroy* the mind, and 20 to debilitate it in innumerable instances. It is equally well known, that the torments of the mind are, in many cases, sufficient to *destroy* the body. This, then, being so well known, is it not the first duty of a father to secure to his children, if possible, sound and strong bodies ? LORD BACON says, that ' a sound mind in a sound body is the greatest of God's blessings.' To see his children possess these, therefore, ought to be the first object with every father ; an object which I cannot too often endeavour to fix in his mind. 30

I am to speak presently of that sort of *learning* which is

L

derived from *books*, and which is a matter by no means to
be neglected, or to be thought little of, seeing that it is the
road, not only to fame, but to the means of doing great
good to one's neighbours and to one's country, and thereby
of adding to those pleasant feelings which are, in other
words, our happiness.   But, notwithstanding this, I must
here insist, and endeavour to impress my opinion upon the
mind of every father, that his children's *happiness* ought
to be his *first* object ;   that *book-learning*, if it tend to
10 militate against this, ought to be disregarded ;   and that,
as to money, as to fortune, as to rank and title, that father
who can, in the destination of his children, think of them
more than of the *happiness* of those children is, if he be of
sane mind, a great criminal.   Who is there, having lived to
the age of thirty, or even twenty, years, and having the
ordinary capacity for observation ;   who is there, being of
this description, who must not be convinced of the in-
adequacy of *riches* and what are called *honours* to insure
happiness ?

On Reading too many Books

(From the *Advice to Young Men*.)

20   WHEN people have nothing useful to do, they may in-
dulge their curiosity ;   but merely to *read books* is not to
be industrious, is not to study, and is not the way to become
learned.   Perhaps there are none more lazy, or more truly
ignorant, than your everlasting readers.   A book is an
admirable excuse for sitting still ;   and a man who has
constantly a newspaper, a magazine, a review, or some
book or other in his hand gets, at last, his head stuffed with
such a jumble that he knows not what to think about any
thing.   An empty coxcomb, that wastes his time in dress-
30 ing, strutting, or strolling about, and picking his teeth, is
certainly a most despicable creature, but scarcely less so

than a mere reader of books, who is, generally, conceited, thinks himself wiser than other men, in proportion to the number of leaves that he has turned over. In short, a young man should bestow his time upon no book the contents of which he cannot apply to some useful purpose.

On History

(From the *Advice to Young Men.*)

To understand well the history of the country, you should first understand how it came to be divided into counties, hundreds, and into parishes ; how judges, sheriffs, and juries first arose ; to what end they were all invented, and how the changes with respect to any of them have been 10 produced. But it is of particular consequence that you ascertain the *state of the people* in former times, which is to be ascertained by *comparing the then price of labour with the then price of food.* You hear enough, and you read enough, about the *glorious wars* in the reign of KING EDWARD the THIRD ; and it is very proper that those glories should be recorded and remembered ; but you never read, in the works of the historians, that, in that reign, a common labourer earned threepence-halfpenny a day ; and that a *fat sheep* was sold, at the same time, for one shilling and twopence, 20 and a fat hog, two years old, for three shillings and four-pence, and a fat goose for twopence-halfpenny. You never read that women received a penny a day for hay-making or weeding in the corn, and that a gallon of red wine was sold for fourpence. These are matters which historians have deemed to be beneath their notice ; but they are matters of real importance : they are matters which ought to have practical effect at this time ; for these furnish the criterion whereby we are to judge of our condition compared with that of our forefathers. The poor-rates form a great feature 30 in the laws and customs of this country. Put to a thousand

persons who have read what is called the history of England ;
put to them the question, how the poor-rates came ? and
nine hundred and ninety-nine of the thousand will tell you,
that they know nothing at all of the matter. This is not
history ; a list of battles and a string of intrigues are not
history, they communicate no knowledge applicable to our
present state ; and it really is better to amuse oneself with
an avowed romance, which latter is a great deal worse than
passing one's time in counting the trees.

A Bishop's Grammar
(From *Cobbett's English Grammar*, 1833.)

10   I HAVE before me ' *A Charge delivered to the Clergy
of the Diocese of Winchester, at a primary visitation of
that diocese, by* GEORGE TOMLINE, *D.D., F.R.S., Lord
Bishop of Winchester, Prelate of the Most Noble Order of the
Garter.*' . . . This Bishop, whose name *was* Prettyman,
was the *tutor* of that *William Pitt* who was called the
heaven-born Minister, and a history of whose life has been
written by this Bishop. So that we have here, *a Doctor of
Divinity, a Fellow of the Royal Society,* a *Prelate of the Most
Noble Order of the Garter,* and a *Bishop of one of the richest
20 sees in the whole world,* who, besides, is an *Historian,* and
was *Tutor to a heaven-born Minister.* Let us then see what
sort of *writing* comes from such a source. I could take an
incorrect sentence, I could even take a specimen of downright nonsense, from almost any page of the *Charge.* But,
I shall content myself with the *very first sentence of it.*

' My Reverend Brethren, being called to preside over this distinguished Diocese at a late period of life, I have thought it incumbent upon me not to delay the opportunity of becoming personally
acquainted with my Clergy longer than circumstances rendered
30 absolutely necessary.'

There are *two* double meanings in this short sentence.
Was he called at some former time, to preside over the
diocese *when he should become old ?* or, was he, *when he had*

become old, called to preside over the diocese ?   But what follows is still worse.   Does he mean that he thought it incumbent on him to become acquainted with his Clergy *as soon as possible*, or, *as short a time as possible ?*   To *delay* an *opportunity* is not very good ;   and that which is of a man's own appointment and which proceeds purely from his own will, cannot strictly be called an *opportunity*.   But, it is the double meaning, occasioned by the *wrong-placing* of the words, that I wish you to attend to. . . .   I dare say that he corrected and re-corrected every sentence of this 10 Charge.   And yet what *bungling* work it is, after all.   And these are your *college* and *university* bred men !

On the Education of the Labouring Man
(From *Cottage Economy*.)

UNDERSTAND me clearly here, however ;   for it is the duty of parents to give, if they be able, book-learning to their children, having *first* taken care to make them capable of earning their living by *bodily labour*.   When that object has once been secured, the other may, if the ability remain, be attended to.   But I am wholly against children wasting their time in the idleness of what is called *education ;*   and particularly in schools over which the parents have no 20 control, and where nothing is taught but the rudiments of servility, pauperism, and slavery.

The *education* that I have in view is, therefore, of a very different kind.   You should bear constantly in mind that nine-tenths of us are, from the very nature and necessities of the world, born to gain our livelihood by the sweat of our brow.   What reason have we, then, to presume that our children are not to do the same ?   If they be, as now and then one will be, endued with extraordinary powers of mind, those powers may have an opportunity of developing them- 30 selves ;   and, if they never have that opportunity, the harm is not very great to us or to them.   Nor does it hence follow

that the descendants of labourers are *always* to be labourers.
The path upwards is steep and long, to be sure. Industry,
care, skill, excellence in the present parent lays the foundation of a *rise*, under more favourable circumstances, for
his children. The children of these take *another rise;* and,
by and by, the descendants of the present labourer become
gentlemen.

This is the natural progress. It is by attempting to reach
the top at a *single leap* that so much misery is produced in
the world; and the propensity to make such attempts has
been cherished and encouraged by the strange projects that
we have witnessed of late years for making the labourers
virtuous and *happy* by giving them what is called *education.*
The education which I speak of consists in bringing children
up to labour with *steadiness*, with *care*, and with *skill;* to
show them how to do as many useful things as possible;
to teach them to do them all in the best manner; to set
them an example in industry, sobriety, cleanliness and
neatness; to make all these *habitual* to them, so that they
never shall be liable to fall into the contrary; to let them
always see a *good living* proceeding from *labour*, and thus
to remove from them the temptation to get at the goods of
others by violent or fraudulent means, and to keep far from
their minds all the inducements to hypocrisy and deceit.

And bear in mind that if the state of the labourer has its
disadvantages when compared with other callings and
conditions of life, it has also its advantages. It is free from
the torments of ambition, and from a great part of the
causes of ill-health, for which not all the riches in the world
and all the circumstances of high rank are a compensation.
The able and prudent labourer is always *safe*, at the least;
and that is what few men are who are lifted above him.
They have losses and crosses to fear, the very thought of
which never enters his mind, if he act well his part towards
himself, his family, and his neighbour.

Temperance

(From the *Advice to Young Men.*)

DESPICABLE are those who suffer any part of their happiness to depend upon what they have to eat or to drink, provided they have *a sufficiency of wholesome food;* despicable is the *man,* and worse than despicable the *youth,* that would make any sacrifice, however small, whether of money or of time, or of anything else, in order to secure a dinner different from that which he would have had without such sacrifice.   Who, what man, ever performed a greater quantity of labour than I have performed ? What man ever did so much ?   Now, in a great measure, I owe my 10 capability to perform this labour to my disregard of dainties. . . . I am certain that, upon an average, I have not, during my life, spent more than *thirty-five minutes a day at table,* including all the meals of the day. I like, and I take care to have, good and clean victuals ; but, if wholesome and clean, that is enough. If I find it, by chance, *too coarse* for my appetite, I put the food aside, or let somebody do it, and leave the appetite to gather keenness. But the great security of all is to eat *little,* and to drink nothing that *intoxicates.* He that eats till he is *full* is little better than 20 a beast ; and he that drinks till he is *drunk* is quite a beast.

Early Rising

(From *Cobbett's Sermons* : *The Sluggard,* 1822.)

To lag in bed is against nature. The whole of the animals of the creation rise when they have had a sufficiency of *rest.* None of them *live in bed.* And, except in cases where their security or the obtaining of their food absolutely requires them to retire to rest in the day time, they rise, at all times of the year, with the sun, or before him. We cannot see in the dark. Few things can be done in darkness.

The day is the time for us to be awake and to be active, and for us to take air. The body and the mind stand in need of repose during the twenty four hours ; and nature as well as reason point out to us that the night is the time for that repose.

As to *health*, it is, in the true sense of the word, wholly unknown to the Sluggard. He may exist in an absence of acute pain ; a naturally good constitution may even give him long life ; but still he cannot enjoy that which is worthy of the name of health. The morning air is the great envigorator of the body and sustainer of the animal spirit. Whether in towns or in the country, the morning, the three first hours after the dawn of day, is the time to breathe the air freely. What life, what animation, activity and gaiety do we perceive, in all living creatures, *early in the morning*, compared with their state at the setting of the sun. What a difference do we ourselves feel in the air of the morning, if we then rise, compared with that which we meet if we rise when the sun is three hours high !

Let it not be imagined, that, so that we pass only *a certain number of hours* in bed, it is no matter, as to our health, of what part of the twenty four they consist. It matters very much. The morning air braces the nerves, strengthens the frame, and keeps the mind clear. By lengthening our day at the other end, we lose that which is to be found only at sun-rise and a short time after. The body and mind mutually act upon each other. The pleasures which the morning affords to the mind assist in giving force to the frame ; and that force communicates itself to the mind. Even drunkards, who have been early risers, have had long life ; but such as have been Sluggards as well as drunkards have seldom lived out half their days.

However, though life is precious with health, and though without health it is worth little, it is in a moral point of view that early rising is of the most importance. He who does not rise early can never make any great exertion for any length of time. It can be in few cases that a man does that *at once*, which is to decide his fate in life. His fortune, his fame, his means of existence even, must generally depend on often-repeated, or long-continued exertion. There must be, in the greater part of cases, a series of acts ; a trial of perseverance. Of how much importance is it, then, to crowd as many acts and as much effect as possible into the space of every day ?

Boxing

(From the *Political Register*, August 1805.)

As few persons will be inclined to believe it possible so far to work, by any human laws, such a change in the hearts and minds of men as shall prevent all quarrelling amongst them, it is not necessary to insist that, in spite of the law and the Gospel, in spite of the animadversions of the bench and the admonitions of the pulpit, there will still be prac- tised some mode or other of terminating quarrels, some way in which the party injured, or offended, will seek for satisfaction, without waiting for the operation of the law, even in those cases where the law affords the means whereby satisfaction is to be obtained. If this be not denied, it will remain with the innovating foes of the pugilistick combat to show that there are other modes of terminating quarrels amongst the common people less offensive to the principles of sound morality, less dangerous in their physical effects, better calculated to produce the restoration of harmony, to shorten the duration, and to prevent the extension, of re- sentment, together with all the evils attendant upon a long- harboured spirit of revenge. Without proceeding another step, I am confident that the reflecting reader, though he may for a moment have been carried away by the cry of *' brutality '*, latterly set up against boxing, will, from our thus simply stating what our opponents have to prove, have clearly perceived that the proof is not within their power. He will have perceived that, of all the ways in which violence can possibly be committed (and violence of some sort there must be in the obtaining of personal satisfaction), none has in it so little hostility to the principles of our religion, and that none is so seldom fatal to the parties, as boxing. He will have perceived, too, that this mode, by excluding the aid of every thing extraneous, by allowing of no weapons, by leaving nothing to deceit, and very little to art of any sort, is, in most cases, decisive as to the powers of the combatants, and proceeds, besides, upon the generous principle that, with the battle, ceases for ever the cause whence it arose ; a principle of such long and steady growth, so deeply rooted in the hearts of Englishmen, that to attempt the revival, or even to allude to, with apparent resentment, the grounds of a quarrel which has been terminated by the fists is always regarded as a mark of baseness, whether visible in the conduct of the parties themselves, or in that of their relations, or friends.

But it is the political view of this subject which appears to me to be most worthy of attention ; the view of the effect which may, by the contemplated change of manners, be produced upon the people, considered as the members of a state, always opposed to some other state ; for, much as I abhor cuttings and stabbings, I have, as I hope most others of my countrymen have, a still greater abhorrence of submission to a foreign yoke.—Commerce, Opulence, Luxury, Effeminacy, Cowardice, Slavery : these are the stages of national degradation. We are in the fourth ; and I beg the reader to consider, to look into history, to trace states in their fall, and then say how rapid is the latter part of the progress ! Of the symptoms of *effeminacy* none is so certain as a change from athletic and hardy sports, or exercises, to those requiring less bodily strength, and

exposing the persons engaged in them to less bodily suffering ; and, when this change takes place, be assured that
national cowardice is at no great distance, the general
admiration of deeds of hardihood having already been considerably lessened.   Bravery, as, indeed, the word imports,
consists not in a readiness and a capacity to kill or to hurt,
but in a readiness and a capacity to venture, and to bear the
consequences.   As sports or exercises approach nearer and
nearer to real combats, the greater, in spite of all we can say,
is our admiration of those who therein excel.   Belcher has, 10
by the sons of cant, in every class of life, been held up to us
as a monster, a perfect ruffian ; yet there are very few
persons who would not wish to see Belcher ; few from
whom marks of admiration have not, at some time, been
extorted by his combats ; and scarcely a female Saint,
perhaps, who would not, in her way to the conventicle, or
even during the snuffling there to be heard, take a peep at
him from beneath her hood.   Can as much be said by any
one of those noblemen and gentlemen who have been spending the best years of their lives in dancing by night and 20
playing at cricket by day ?   The reason is, not that Belcher
strikes hard ; not that he is strong ; not that he is an adept
at his art ; but that he exposes himself voluntarily to so
much danger, and that he bears so many heavy blows.   We
are apt to laugh at the preference which women openly give
to soldiers (including, of course, all men of the military
profession), a preference which is always found, too, to be
given by young persons of both sexes.   But, if we take time
to consider, we shall find this partiality to be no fit subject
for ridicule or blame.   It is a partiality naturally arising 30
from the strongest of all feelings, *the love of life*.   The profession of arms is always the most honourable.   All kings
and princes are soldiers.   Renowned soldiers are never
forgotten.   We all talk of Alexander the Great and of Julius
Cæsar ; but very few of us ever heard, or ever thought of

inquiring, what were the statesmen of those days. There is not, perhaps, a ploughman in England, who has not a hundred times repeated the names of Drake and of Marlborough ; and of the hundreds of thousands of them, there is not one, perhaps, who ever heard, or ever will hear, pronounced, the name of Cecil or of Godolphin.

A Sensual Prosperity

(From the *Political Register*, July 9–16, 1803.)

Some parts of the plan now about to be brought forward should have in view the defence of the country at the present time ; but it should have a steady eye to the rendering of the people of this kingdom a *military people*, for a military people we must become, or we must be slaves ; there is no other alternative ; no Sunday schools, no soup-shops, no canting philanthropic societies ; nothing will any longer save us from the use of arms or from the wearing of chains. A law, therefore, which is intended to further this mighty purpose should be maturely considered : it should go slowly through the Cabinet, and still more slowly through the Parliament ; it should receive the aid of all the sagacity and all the experience of the country, and, above all things, it should be founded upon a principle of *longevity*, looking forward, not only to a long war, but to a military age ; not only to our present protection, but to the safety and the honour of our children. ' Carthage,' says Montesquieu, ' which made war with its opulence against the poverty of Rome, laboured, from that cause, under a great disadvantage : gold and silver passeth away ; but the strength and fortitude of poverty nothing can destroy. The Romans were ambitious from *pride*, the Carthaginians from *avarice* ; the one wished to *command*, the other to *acquire* ; and these latter, constantly calculating the *receipt* and *expenditure*, always *sighed for peace while they were making war.* Commercial states may long subsist in *mediocrity* ; but their *grandeur* is of short duration. They rise, little by little, without being perceived : but, when the wealth of such a nation has swelled to a magnitude no longer to be hidden, every other nation seeks to deprive her of that which she has acquired, if not clandestinely, at least without any of those deeds, which constitute the merit of nations.'—Before truths like these how the vaunting estimates of financiers shrink into nothingness ! Duly impressed with those solemn and fearful truths, we turn 10 from Mr. Pitt's 'commercial *greatness*', from the '*splendid* assets' of Lord Castlereagh, from the '*magnificent* receipts' of Lord Auckland, with a loathing hardly to be described. No ; it is neither by *trade* nor by *money* that we can be saved ; but by *men* and *arms* ; and it is a truth that never can be too often repeated that we must become a *military people*, or we must become *slaves*.

A Call to Manhood

(From the *Political Register*, July 1803.)

THE sun, in his whole course round the globe, shines not on a spot so blessed as this great, and now united Kingdom ; gay and productive fields and gardens, lofty and extensive 20 woods, innumerable flocks and herds, rich and inexhaustible mines, a mild and wholesome climate, giving health, activity, and vigour to fourteen millions of people ; and shall we, who are thus favoured and endowed ; shall we, who are abundantly supplied with iron and steel, powder and lead ; shall we, who have a fleet superior to the maritime force of all the world, and who are able to bring two millions of fighting men into the field ; shall we yield up this dear and happy land, together with all the liberties and honours, to preserve which our fathers so often dyed the 30 land and the sea with their blood ; shall we thus at once

dishonour their graves, and stamp disgrace and infamy on the brows of our children ; and shall we, too, make this base and dastardly surrender to an enemy whom, within these twelve years, our countrymen have defeated in every quarter of the world ? No ; we are not so miserably fallen ; we cannot in so short a space of time have become so detestably degenerate : we have the strength and the will to repel the hostility, to chastise the insolence of the foe. Mighty, indeed, must be our efforts, but mighty also is the meed.
10 Singly engaged against the tyrants of the earth, Britain now attracts the eyes and the hearts of mankind ; groaning nations look to her for deliverance ; justice, liberty, and religion are inscribed on her banners ; her success will be hailed with the shouts of the universe, while tears of admiration and gratitude will bedew the heads of her sons, who fall in the glorious contest.

A Call to the Aristocracy

(From the *Political Register*, September 1803.)

THE period is approaching when the descendants of our antient heroes may find the qualities, which brought consideration and honours to their ancestors, again esteemed,
20 and again roused into action. The strength and value of the landed interest will be once more duly appreciated ; and the false splendour of mercantile wealth no longer monopolize the attention of the legislature and the government.

' Whither is Europe's antient spirit fled ?
Where are those valiant tenants of her shore,
Who from the warrior-bow the strong dart sped,
Or with firm hand the rapid pole-axe bore ?
Freeman and soldier was their common name
Who late with reapers to the furrow came :
30 Now in the front of battle charg'd the foe :
Who taught the steer the wint'ry plough to endure :
Now in full councils check'd encroaching power,
And gave the guardian laws their majesty to know.

If I could but see an end to this degrading system of FUNDING and the consequent check which would be given, to the ruinous and revolutionary tricks of the money-market, I should yet hope that our military and substantial power, instead of thus trembling on the edge of annihilation, might be greater than it ever yet has been. But the spirit, which prevailed in the days of the PLANTAGENETS and TUDORS, must revive : distinctions must fall into other channels ; and legislation be delegated to other tongues. The days of the Veres, and Percies, and Cliffords, and 10 Nevilles must return ; and the glory of leading *vassals* into the *field*, instead of bringing the greatest array of *bank-notes* towards the completion of a *loan*, must obtain the smiles of a Monarch and conciliate the regard and admiration of a people.

The Failure of the English Gentleman

(From *Rural Rides*, September 1, 1826.)

FOR my own part, I really am ashamed to ride a fat horse, to have a full belly, and to have a clean shirt upon my back, while I look at these wretched countrymen of mine ; while I actually see them reeling with weakness ; when I see their poor faces present me nothing but skin and bone, while 20 they are toiling to get the wheat and the meat ready to be carried away to be devoured by the tax-eaters. I am ashamed to look at these poor souls, and to reflect that they are my countrymen ; and particularly to reflect that we are descended from those amongst whom ' beef, pork, mutton, and veal, were the food of the poorer sort of people.' . . . We are reversing the maxim of the Scripture : our laws almost say that those that work shall not eat, and that those who do not work shall have the food. I repeat, that the baseness of the English land-owners surpasses that of any 30 other men that ever lived in the world. The cowards know

well that the labourers that give value to their land are skin
and bone. They are not such brutes as not to know that
this starvation is produced by taxation. . . . Sir James
Graham, of Netherby, may invoke our pity upon these
'ancient families,' but he will invoke in vain.   It was
their duty to stand forward and prevent Power-of-Im-
prisonment Bills, Six-Acts, Ellenborough's Act, Poaching
Transportation Act, New Trespass Act, Sunday Tolls, and
the hundreds of other things that could be named. On the
contrary, *they were the cause of them all*. They were the
cause of all the taxes and all the debts ; and now let them
take the consequences !

Poverty and Labour

(From *Cobbett's Sermons : On the Rights of the Poor*, 1821.)

Man, and, indeed, it is the same with every living thing,
delights in *ease*, and labour, though conducive to health,
and, therefore, in the *end*, to pleasure, does, in itself, partake of the nature of *pain ;* it fatigues the body, or the
mind, and, therefore, to cause it to be performed a motive
is requisite, and a motive, too, sufficient to outweigh the
natural love of ease. In proportion as the labour is of a
nature to cause fatigue, to give pain, to place the body in a
state of risk, the motive to undertake and perform it must
be strong. And *the fear of poverty :* that is to say, the fear of
being destitute of food and raiment, appears to be absolutely
necessary to send the savage forth to hunt for the flesh of
the deer and the skin of the bear, and to induce men to
perform all the various functions necessary to their support
in civil society, and not less necessary to the existence of
civil society itself.

This motive is, too, the great source of the virtues and
the pleasures of mankind. Early-rising, sobriety, provident
carefulness, attentive observation, a regard for reputation,

reasoning on causes and effects, skill in the performance of labour, arts, sciences, even public-spirit and military valour and renown, will all be found, at last, to have had their foundation in *a fear of poverty :* and, therefore, it is manifest that the existence of poverty is indispensably necessary, whether a people be in a wild or a civilized state ; because without its existence mankind would be unpossessed of this salutary fear.

But we are not to look upon poverty as necessarily arising from the *fault* of those who are poor, there being 10 so many other causes continually at work to produce poverty amongst every people. The man who is born an idiot, or who has been stricken blind by lightning, and who, in consequence of either of these calamities, is destitute of the means of obtaining food and raiment, is poor without any *fault.* Feebleness of frame, ailments of the body, distress of mind, may all produce poverty without fault in the afflicted party. There may be misfortunes, the impoverishing effects of which no human industry, care, or foresight could have prevented. Poverty may arise from the faults 20 of parents. In all such cases the poor are clearly entitled to the compassion, the tender consideration, the active charity, out of which relief instantly springs. Nay, even when poverty manifestly proceeds from unhappy disposition, from untractable temper, from our own passions, it ought not to be visited with a very severe chastisement. And, as to starvation and nakedness, they are too heavy a punishment for any *crime* short of wilful murder. . . .

The great corrective of the insolence of riches is to be found in tracing them back to their source ; that is to say, 30 *to the labour of the poor.* This is the source of all riches ; for, if the labourer received, at all times, the full value of his labour, no profit could arise from it to any other person. All the profit would remain with himself, and no one would be puffed up into riches. It is not contended that this

ought to be ; because the order of the world requires that there should be motives to exertion ; and these motives are the hope of riches and the fear of poverty. But a state of things may arise when men are not content with moderate riches ; and this may lead to oppressions which may in time destroy the fear of poverty, which may in short make the labourer worse than a bondman ; make him a slave ; make him the property of his employer; hang the lash over his back and deprive him of all fear but of that. Un-
10 happy, indeed, is a people reduced to a state like this. The name of *poor* is in such a case hardly applicable ; and, indeed, the word poor does not belong, in reason, to the labourer. The state of the labourer is merely one of the links in the chain of society : it is one of the ranks of society ; and, rightly viewed, it is by no means the lowest. All property has its origin in labour. Labour itself is property; the root of all other property; and unhappy is that community, where labourer and poor man are synonymous terms. . . .

20   In order to disguise from ourselves our own meanness, ingratitude and cruelty, we put the thing on a different footing : we consider labour as an article of *merchandise*, and then proceed upon the maxim that we have a right to purchase as cheap as we can. This maxim, even supposing the idea of merchandise to be correct, is not so sound as habit, and very vicious habit, makes us regard it to be. We are not justified, upon any principle of morality, to give less for any thing than we ourselves believe the thing to be worth, because this is not doing as we would be done
30 unto. The comparison, therefore, is of little avail ; and besides, a worse example than that of the merchant could not easily be referred to.

'He is a *Merchant*,' says the Prophet Hosea, 'the balances of deceit are in his hand ; he loveth to *oppress*.' No wonder that those who wish to enrich themselves by the means of unjust profits drawn from labour should put themselves

upon the footing of the Merchant.   But labour is not
merchandise, except, indeed, it be the labour of a slave.
It is altogether personal.   It is inseparable from the body
of the labourer ; and cannot be considered as an article to
be cheapened, without any regard being had to the well-
being of the person who has to perform it.   The labourer,
if you persist in treating his labour as a commodity for which
you have a right to give the smallest quantity of food in
return, has his rights, too ; his rights of nature ; his right
to a sufficiency of food and of raiment; or else his right ₁₀
to employ his strength and ingenuity to obtain them without reference to the laws passed for the appropriation of
the property created by labour.

The Labourer and the Land

(From *A Legacy to Labourers*, published 1834.)

WHAT was the ground stated for uprooting (by the Poor
Law Amendment Act of 1834) the old and amiable
parochial governments of England . . . for sweeping away
this government carried on by neighbours for their mutual
good and happiness ? . . .

Long before the Norman Conquest all the lands were
charged with tithes, out of which tithes the law required ₂₀
that the poor should be relieved. . . . But the change of
religion [at the Reformation] and the transfer of the tithes
and of the estates of the monasteries caused the tithe-
owners and the new abbey-landholders to *neglect* this sacred
part of their duty, the relieving of the poor.   They cast aside
this duty by degrees : the people complained of this
robbery committed upon them ; and . . . an Act of
Parliament was passed in the forty-third year of Elizabeth
providing effectually for their relief . . . ; and this law
continued in force, and a happy and kind people lived ₃₀
under it for nearly two hundred years. . . . The *poor-rates*
were no more than a *compensation* for what had been with-

held from the people by the injustice of the Protestant
clergy and the landlords. . . .

Without the labourer the land is nothing worth. Without
his labour there can be no tillage, no inclosure of fields, no
tending of flocks, no breeding of animals, and a farm is
worth no more than an equal number of acres of the sea or
of the air. It is the labour that causes the rents. Therefore
the labouring people, whether in sickness or in health, are
to have the first maintenance out of the land. Tell me not
10 that the farmer is unable to yield to the labourers their
rights. In the very nature of things he must have ability
to provide them with a sufficiency ; because his land produces ten times as much as they can consume.

Pastoral Christianity

(From *A History of the Protestant Reformation*, published 1824-7.)

THEN look at the monasteries as causing, in some of the
most important of human affairs, that fixedness which is so
much the friend of rectitude in morals, and which so power-
fully conduces to prosperity, private and public. The
monastery was a proprietor that never died ; its tenantry
had to do with a deathless landlord ; its lands and houses
20 never changed owners; its tenants were liable to none of the
many uncertainties that other tenants were; its oaks
had never to tremble at the axe of the squandering heir ;
its manors had not to dread a change of lords; its villagers
had all been born and bred up under its eye and care ; their
character was of necessity a thing of great value, and, as
such, would naturally be an object of great attention. A
monastery was the centre of a circle in the country, naturally drawing to it all that were in need of relief, advice, and
protection, and containing a body of men or of women
30 having no cares of their own, and having wisdom to guide
the inexperienced and wealth to relieve the distressed.

And was it a good thing, then, to plunder and devastate these establishments : was it a reformation to squander estates thus employed upon lay persons, who would not, who could not, and did not, do any part or particle of those benevolent facts and acts of public utility which naturally arose out of the monastic institutions ?

Lastly, let us look at the monasteries as a resource for the younger sons and daughters of the aristocracy, and as the means of protecting the government against the injurious effects of their clamorous wants. There cannot exist an aristocracy or body of nobility without the means, in the hands of the government, of preventing that body from falling into that contempt which is, and always must be, inseparable from noble poverty. ' Well,' some will say, ' why need there be any such body ?' That is quite another question : for we have it, and have had it for more than a thousand years ; except during a very short interval, at the end of which our ancestors eagerly took it back again. I must, too, though it really has nothing to do with the question before us, repeat my opinion, many times expressed, that we should lose more than we should gain by getting rid of our aristocracy.

Nor must we by any means overlook the effects of those institutions on the mere face of the country. That soul must be low and mean indeed which is insensible to all feeling of pride in the noble edifices of its country. Love of country, that variety of feelings which all together constitute what we properly call patriotism, consists in part of the admiration of and veneration for ancient and magnificent proofs of skill and of opulence. The monastics built as well as wrote for posterity. The never-dying nature of their institutions set aside, in all their undertakings, every calculation as to time and age. Whether they built or planted, they set the generous example of providing for the pleasure, the honour, the wealth and greatness of genera-

tions upon generations yet unborn. They executed every thing in the very best manner : their gardens, fishponds, farms,—in all, in the whole of their economy, they set an example tending to make the country beautiful, to make it an object of pride with the people, and to make the nation truly and permanently great. Go into any county, and survey, even at this day, the ruins of its perhaps twenty abbeys and priories, and then ask yourself, 'what have we in exchange for these?' Go to the site of some once opulent convent.
10 Look at the cloister, now become in the hands of a rack-renter the receptacle for dung, fodder and faggot-wood ; see the hall, where for ages the widow, the orphan, the aged and the stranger found a table ready spread; see a bit of its walls now helping to make a cattle-shed, the rest having been hauled away to build a workhouse ; recognize in the side of a barn a part of the once magnificent chapel ; and if, chained to the spot by your melancholy musings, you be admonished of the approach of night by the voice of the screech-owl issuing from those arches which once at the same
20 hour resounded with the vespers of the monk, and which have for seven hundred years been assailed by storms and tempests in vain,—if thus admonished of the necessity of seeking food, shelter, and a bed, lift your eyes and look at the whitewashed and dry-rotten shell on the hill, called the ' gentleman's house ', and apprised of the ' board wages ' and the ' spring guns ', suddenly turn your head ; jog away from the scene of devastation ; with ' old English hospitality ' in your mind reach the nearest inn, and there, in room half-warmed and half-lighted, and with reception
30 precisely proportioned to the presumed length of your purse, sit down and listen to an account of the hypocritical pretences, the base motives, the tyrannical and bloody means under which, from which, and by which that devastation was effected and that hospitality banished for ever from the land.

The True Reformer

(From the *Advice to Young Men*.)

IF the right to have a share in making the laws were
merely a feather; if it were a fanciful thing; if it were only
a speculative theory; if it were but an *abstract principle*:
on any of these suppositions, it might be considered as of
little importance. But it is none of these; it is a practical
matter; the want of it not only *is*, but must of necessity
be, felt by every man who lives under that want. The
natural and inevitable consequences of a want of this right
in the people have, in all countries, been *taxes* pressing the
industrious and laborious to the earth; *severe laws* and
standing armies to compel the people to submit to those
taxes; wealth, luxury, and splendour, amongst those who
make the laws and receive the taxes; poverty, misery,
immorality and crime, amongst those who bear the burdens;
and at last commotion, revolt, revenge, and rivers of blood.
Such have always been, and such must always be, the consequences of a want of this right of all men to share in the
making of the laws, a right, as I have before shown, derived
immediately from the law of Nature, springing up out of
the same source with civil society, and cherished in the
heart of man by reason and by experience. . . .

Amongst the virtues of the good Citizen are those of
fortitude and patience; and, when he has to carry on his
struggle against corruptions deep and widely-rooted, he
is not to expect the baleful tree to come down at a single
blow; he must patiently remove the earth that props and
feeds it, and sever the accursed roots one by one. . . .What
does the *real* patriot want more than to feel conscious that
he has done his duty towards his country; and that, if life
should not allow him time to see his endeavours crowned
with success, his children will see it? The impatient

patriots are like the young men (mentioned in the beautiful fable of LA FONTAINE) who ridiculed the man of fourscore, who was planting an avenue of very small trees, which, they told him that he never could expect to see as high as his head. 'Well,' said he, 'and what of that ? If their shade afford me no pleasure, it may afford pleasure to my children, and even to you · and, therefore, the planting of them gives me pleasure.'

NOTES

PAGE 1, l. 2. *Cribb*, Tom (1781–1848), champion pugilist.

l. 5. *fillips the ear*, &c. : 2 *Henry IV*, I. ii. 259.

l. 16. *Mandeville*, Bernard (1670 ?–1733), author of *The Fable of the Bees* (1714).

PAGE 2, l. 4. *Paine*, Tom (1737–1809), inspirited the American armies in the War of Independence with his *Common Sense* (1776) and other writings ; supported the French Revolution in *The Rights of Man* (1790) ; and assailed Christianity in *The Age of Reason* (1793).

l. 22. *damnable iteration :* I *Henry IV*, I. ii. 101.

l. 23. *Erskine*, Thomas (1750–1823), Lord Chancellor 1806–7.

PAGE 4, l. 7. *caviare to the Whigs :* cf. *Hamlet*, II. ii. 466.

l. 12. *nunquam sufflaminandus.* From M. Annaeus Seneca, *Controversiae* 4 praef. § 7 : Itaque D. Augustus optime dixit, Aterius noster sufflaminandus est, ' has to be checked '. Applied to Shakespeare by Ben Jonson in his *Discoveries*.

l. 16. *weary, stale*, &c. : *Hamlet*, I. ii. 133.

PAGE 5, l. 7. *the Barmecide.* See the Barber's story of his sixth brother in *The Arabian Nights*.

l. 20. *account of his first breakfast :* *Political Register*, Saturday, July 12, 1817.

l. 23. *paints . . . the plumage : A Year's Residence in the United States of America*, § 22.

l. 25. *groves of the Ohio.* Hazlitt seems to be taking for Cobbett's own an account by a Mr. Hulme of a visit to the valley of the Ohio included in *A Year's Residence.*

l. 27. *turnips.* See *A Year's Residence* (2nd ed.), p. 94.

l. 31. *Bewick*, Thomas (1753–1828), wood-engraver, best known by his *General History of Quadrupeds* (1790) and *History of British Birds* (1797, 1804).

l. 33. *Parr*, Samuel (1747–1825), schoolmaster and divine, an eminent Whig writer, famous for his personal mannerisms.

l. 34. *Mr. ——.* Probably Henry Brougham, Lord Chancellor, 1830–4, whom Cobbett assailed as a Whig, e. g., in the *Political Register*, June 1, 1816.

PAGE 6, l. 23. *Yanguesian carriers.* See *Don Quixote*, I. iii. xv.

l. 24. *He has the back-trick*, &c. : *Twelfth Night*, I. iii. 133.

l. 28. *arrowy sleet : Paradise Regained*, iii. 323–5.

PAGE 7, l. 25. *an Ishmaelite indeed :* cf. Genesis xvi. 12, and St. John i. 47.

PAGE 9, l. 21. *two-penny trash : Political Register*, August 1817.

PAGE **10**, l. 33. *ample scope*, &c. : Gray, *The Bard*, ii. 1 :
' Give ample room and verge enough.'

PAGE **11**, l. 6. *tosses and tumbles about his unwieldy bulk*,
from Burke's *A Letter to a Noble Lord*, on the Duke of Bedford
wallowing in the royal bounty.

l. 22. *He pours out all*, &c.: Pope, *Imitations of Horace*,
Sat. II. i. 51–2.

PAGE **12**, l. 8. *Antipholis of Ephesus : Comedy of Errors*,
v. i.

l. 10. *bringing over the relics.* See p. xv.

l. 23. *his canonized bones :* Hamlet, I. iv. 47.

PAGE **13**, l. 19. *The Edinburgh Review . . . dead set at him :*
in an article by Jeffrey in July 1807, answered in *The Political
Register* in August.

PAGE **14**, l. 24. *Walker the Original.* Thomas Walker (1784–
1836), a London police magistrate, published his thoughts on
society and morals in a weekly paper entitled *The Original*
during some months of 1835. It contained admirable articles
on gastronomy and health.

PAGE **15**, l. 23. *Werterism.* The hero of Goethe's romance,
The Sorrows of Werther (*Die Thränen des jungen Werther*), is
a ' beautiful soul ' who takes his own life under the disappoint-
ment of an impracticable passion.

l. 26. *These men were made in England : Henry V*, III. ii. 26.

PAGE **16**, l. 13. *De Rochefoucault.* In the first edition of his
Maximes, 1665, No. 99, François de Marsillac, Duc de La
Rochefoucauld (1613–80), said that ' dans l'adversité de nos
meilleurs amis nous trouvons toujours quelque chose qui ne
nous déplaît pas '.

PAGE **17**, l. 11. *Bradford*, the son of a bookseller in Philadelphia. Cobbett quarrelled with father and son in 1796.

l. 25. *Prosperity Robinson :* Frederick John, Viscount
Goderich, and later Earl of Ripon (1782–1859). He proposed
the corn duty of 1815, and as Chancellor of the Exchequer
(1823–7) introduced many fiscal reforms.

Oeolus Canning : George (1770–1827), Foreign Secretary
at various times. He supported the Liberal causes abroad and
the coercion at home.

l. 26. *Liverpool :* Robert Banks Jenkinson, second Earl
(1770–1828), Prime Minister, 1812–27.

PAGE **18**, l. 18. 1809 is the date of Cobbett's imprisonment ;
1822 that of the death of Castlereagh. The last prosecution
against the *Register* was in 1831.

PAGE **19**, l. 10. *gloated over the circumstances.* See the *Letter
to Joseph Swann*, *Register*, August 1822, quoted in Carlyle's
Cobbett, p. 241. Robert Stewart, Viscount Castlereagh (1769–
1822), one of the dominant statesmen during and after the
war, committed suicide under the stress of responsibility.

NOTES

l. 17. *Wilkes*, John (1727–97), leader of the Radical agitation under George III.

PAGE **20**, l. 23.   *Arthur Young* (1741–1820), author of numerous works on English agriculture, from 1767.

PAGE **21**, l. 25.   *Thomas Robert Malthus* (1766–1834), author of the *Essay on Population* (1798), and *Edwin Chadwick* (1800–90), social reformer and civil servant, were prominent supporters of the Poor Law Amendment Act, 1834, which confined the able-bodied paupers to workhouses.

l. 27.   *poor-law of Elizabeth*, in 1601, putting the duty of relief on the parishes.

PAGE **22**, l. 8.   *this system*, i. e. of out-door relief, often a supplement to wages. See note to p. 113.

l. 11.   Malthus was in favour of withholding relief from all but the old and impotent, as in Scotland.

PAGE **25**, l. 12.   *Peter Pindar*, pseudonym used by John Wolcot (1738–1819), satirist.

l. 14.   *Junius.* A number of letters under this pseudonym in *The Public Advertiser* between November 1768 and January 1772 fiercely assailed the Court and Parliament of the day. The author is supposed to have been Philip Francis, the adversary of Warren Hastings.

l. 27.   *Ailie Dinmont*, wife of Dandie, in *Guy Mannering*.

PAGE **27**.   *Ebenezer Elliott* (1781–1849), the poet of the corn-law agitation (*Corn-Law Rhymes*, published in 1831).

SELECTIONS FROM COBBETT

PAGE **30**.   *The Life and Adventures of Peter Porcupine*.   This autobiographical fragment, published at Philadelphia, was written to prove to Americans that his Tory principles did not come from aristocratic prejudices imbibed in youth.

l. 7.   *William Penn* (1644–1718), who founded Pennsylvania in 1682, primarily as a land of refuge for Quakers and deists, was born and bred and died in England.

PAGE **31**, l. 1. *Franklin*, Benjamin (1706–90), the discoverer of the lightning-conductor, and champion of American freedom, a deist, and at one time a free-thinker. He was the son of a soap-maker and became a printer, published a popular Almanac, acted as American ambassador in Paris, and wrote an uncompleted autobiography. He advocated vegetarianism, contributed to medical science, and devised improvements in chimneys, and also in Leyden jars, among many other inventions ; and he was founder of a library and a hospital in Philadelphia. He was lax in morals, and his marriage was of doubtful validity.

PAGE **36**, l. 22.   *Rodney's victories*, at Cape St. Vincent over the Spaniards in 1780, and over the French fleet in the West Indies in April 1782.

PAGE **37,** l. 22. *Mr. Swanwick.* This is probably a sneer. John Swanwick represented Philadelphia in Congress on the democratic side, and was in Cobbett's bad books.

PAGE **40,** l. 17. *John Doe and Richard Roe,* conventional terms for the opposing parties in a suit.

PAGE **41,** l. 8. *Gil Blas.* This work, a masterpiece in the humorous romance of adventure, by Alain René Lesage (1668–1747), began to appear in 1715, and was finished in 1735. The reference is to Book I, iv–x.

PAGE **43,** l. 6. *Sir William Temple* (1628–99), statesman and essayist, employed Swift as his private secretary for some five years between 1692 and 1699.

PAGE **44,** l. 14. *hautboys,* a tall species of strawberry.

PAGE **49,** l. 22. *Nootka Sound,* between the islands of Nootka and Vancouver. In 1790, Spain, resenting an English settlement on this Sound, was prevented from going to war by the refusal of France to join with her.

l. 26. *Lord Edward Fitzgerald,* one of the arch-conspirators of the Irish rising of 1798, died of a wound received at his arrest.

PAGE **62,** l. 24. *Duquesnois.* He probably means François Quesnay (1694–1774), founder of the physiocratic theory of political economy, and personal physician to Louis XV.

PAGE **63,** l. 9. *Sidmouth :* Henry Addington, Viscount Sidmouth (1757–1844), Home Secretary from 1812 to 1821.

PAGE **66,** l. 32. *Gibbs,* Sir Vicary, Attorney-General, 1807–12, afterwards Chief Justice of Common Pleas.

Ellenborough : Edward Law, first Baron Ellenborough, Lord Chief Justice from 1802 to 1818.

PAGE **67,** l. 1. *Perceval,* Spencer, Prime Minister from 1809 to 1812, when he was assassinated.

PAGE **70,** l. 13. The names in this paragraph are those of Sussex farmers. Cobbett had reflected in the *Register* on their treatment of labour.

PAGE **71,** l. 10. *the Wen,* i. e. London.

l. 14. *the Gridiron.* On the passing, in 1819, of Peel's Bill for the resumption of cash payments, Cobbett prophesied that it could not take full and immediate effect, and that the nation would be crushed by paying in gold a debt negotiated in paper. He offered, if his prophecy were falsified, to allow Lord Castlereagh ' to put me on a gridiron and broil me alive, while Sidmouth stirs the fire, and Canning stands by, making a jest of my groans ' ; and often put a woodcut of a gridiron on the front page of the *Register* to advertise his promise.

l. 16. *a million of trees.* This apparently means a million trees growing on his own farm or in other places from slips taken thence. He used the *Register* to advertise his locust-trees, of which he sold nearly 14,000 roots to Lord Folkestone at a single deal.

l. 22. *Six-Acts :* six bills, conferring extraordinary powers for dealing with the agents of sedition, passed in November and December of 1819.

l. 25. *Power of Imprisonment :* the suspension of the Habeas Corpus Act in 1817.

l. 26. *his Circular :* to the lord-lieutenants, authorizing magistrates to apprehend persons accused of libellous publications, March 1817.

Letter of Thanks, after they had suppressed a riot at Manchester (Peterloo) in August 1819.

PAGE **72.** The debate was on a Bill to regulate the naturalization of foreigners.

l. 15. *Madison*, James (1751–1836), a leader of the Democrats and afterwards fourth President of the United States.

PAGE **75** l. 3. *five thousand dollars at a time :* the damages assessed by the jury for his libel on Rush in December 1799.

PAGE **76** l. 4. *Give me*, &c. Proverbs xxx. 8. By ' Hagar ' he means Agur, ibid. xxx. 1.

PAGE **80**, l. 1. *Decatur, Hull, and Brainbridge*, American naval commanders in the war of 1812–14.

l. 5. *Lord Cochrane :* Thomas, afterwards Earl of Dundonald (1775–1860), one of the greatest of the British admirals, a fearless critic of government, and a friend of Cobbett's.

l. 6. *Cashman*, a sailor executed in 1817 as a ringleader in a London riot. It was proved that he had come to London to apply for arrears of pay and prize-money.

l. 12. *Jackson*, Andrew (1767–1845), seventh President of the United States. He commanded the American Army in the war of 1812–14, and defeated the British attempt on New Orleans made in 1815 in ignorance of the conclusion of peace.

PAGE **81.** Burghclere lies under the north Hampshire hills, and is about midway between Newbury and Whitchurch.

PAGE **82.** Everley is on the downs between the Vale of Pewsey and Salisbury Plain, some three miles north-west of Ludgershall.

PAGE **85.** Hurstbourn Tarrant is almost due north of Andover.

PAGE **87,** l. 11. *Bower*, the name of a couple of houses close to Froxfield, which is west-north-west of Petersfield.

PAGE **89,** l. 1. He is looking eastward from the top of the hanger over the valley in which Hawkley lies. The two promontories are to the north of him.

l. 10. *round, eastward, to the north*, i. e. the east side of the valley.

PAGE **89,** l. 13. *to the north-west,* i. e. of the heaths.

PAGE **93,** l. 16. *Evelyn,* John (1620–1706), the diarist. His *Sylva* (1664) was a plea for replanting deforested areas.

PAGE **97,** l. 3. *Richard,* his son.

l. 11. This seems to allude to the beauty of the site of Coburg, and to the two ducal palaces and pleasure-grounds in its neighbourhood, Kallenberg and Rosenau.

PAGE **98,** l. 24. *Tilford Green,* three miles south-east of Farnham.

PAGE **99,** l. 16. *Shepry,* Sheppey.

PAGE **104,** l. 2. *Barn-Elm,* in Barnes, east Surrey.

PAGE **105.** *Orcop,* nine miles south-south-west of Hereford.

PAGE **106,** l. 17. *Esham,* i. e. Evesham, locally ' Esam '.

PAGE **109,** l. 21. *a septennial parliament.* Till the Seven Years' Parliament, which carried through the severance from Rome, met in 1529, no Parliament had sat longer than one year.

PAGE **110,** l. 24. *New-church Act.* In 1818 Parliament voted £1,000,000 to build new churches.

l. 30. *by taxes wrung by force.* The rebuilding of St. Paul's after the Great Fire was begun in 1675, and paid for by subscriptions and by an annual tax on coal.

PAGE **112,** l. 21. *a people of plain and good manners.* ' A people who preserve more of the original English simplicity and purity of manners than perhaps any other ' (Burke, on the people of Bristol, *Letter to the Sheriffs of Bristol,* 1777).

PAGE **113,** l. 5. *allowed wages.* The system from 1795 to 1834 was to supplement wages, if necessary, by an allowance from the rates up to a minimum standard, which was, as a rule, that fixed by the Berkshire magistrates at a meeting at Speenhamland, now a part of Newbury, in 1795. The rate was professedly determined by the price of corn. This man got 11*d.* + 7*d.* a day.

PAGE **118,** l. 24. *Ireland's lazy root.* Cobbett had a hearty prejudice against potatoes as a debilitating food.

PAGE **119,** l. 9. *Avington,* some four miles north-east of Winchester.

l. 29. *descendant of Rollo,* i. e. of the Normans.

PAGE **123,** l. 16. *Westborough Green,* Wisborough Green, near Petworth.

PAGE **126,** l. 8. *Hambledon,* on the Meon, a few miles south of Bishops Waltham in Hampshire.

PAGE **127,** l. 12. *rivulet of Whitchurch,* the site of the mill that produced the paper for bank-notes. The Bank of England was established in 1694.

l. 20. *Baron Maseres :* Francis Maseres (1731–1824), Cursitor Baron of the Exchequer and judge of London sheriffs' court ; mathematician and reformer ; of a Huguenot family. He visited Cobbett, when in prison, in his judge's robes, to do him honour.

PAGE **128,** l. 1. *Duchess of Marlborough :* Sarah (1660–1744), wife of the first duke.

l. 11. *Sir William Temple.* See note to p. 43.

l. 18. *William of Wykham,* i. e. Wykeham (1324–1404), Bishop of Winchester and Chancellor of England, endowed and built Winchester College, and founded New College, Oxford.

l. 24. *Alexander Baring* (1774–1848), first Baron Ashburton, son of Sir Francis, the founder of the financial house.

l. 25. *the Duke of Bolton :* Harry Paulet, sixth duke (1719–94), admiral.

l. 29. The first Earl of Northington, Robert Henley (1708–72), was Lord Chancellor ; the second, of the same name (1747–86), was a Lord-Lieutenant of Ireland.

l. 30. *Thomas Baring* (1799–1873), financier.

PAGE **129,** l. 23. *Graham,* Sir James (1792–1861), Whig statesman, with a keen interest in agriculture and the rural classes.

PAGE **131,** l. 29. *bat,* officer's baggage.

PAGE **133,** l. 16. *according to the ancient law.* Tithe, as Cobbett continually insisted, was originally a tax in part for the maintenance of the poor, in part for that of the bishop, the incumbent, and the fabric of the Church. The bishop's claim was cancelled when the bishoprics were endowed. The partial right of the poor in the tithes was last affirmed by Acts under Richard II and Henry IV. After this it silently lapsed, and was not considered when, at the Reformation, great masses of tithe property passed into secular hands.

PAGE **134,** l. 9. *Norton Bovant . . . Bishopstrow.* See p. 81.

l. 18. *Ottiwell Wood :* father of the member for Preston, whom he financed. See next note.

PAGE **135,** l. 5. *the 'individual' :* the Hon. E. G. Stanley, afterwards Earl of Derby, who, with a merchant named John Wood, was elected for Preston in 1826, Cobbett being an unsuccessful candidate. The crowd spat upon Stanley when entering the town to open the campaign (*Political Register,* June 8, 1826).

l. 35. *George Chalmers* (1742–1825), antiquary and editor.

PAGE **145,** l. 25. *Lord Bacon.* Not in the *Essays.* The source is Juvenal x. 356.

PAGE **150,** l. 11. *strange projects.* The modern movement to primary education began at the close of the eighteenth century, and many schools were built and staffed, either by the National Society, representing the Church and directed by Andrew Bell, or by the British and Foreign Schools Society, representing

the Dissenters and directed by Joseph Lancaster. The first
Government subsidy was granted in 1832.

PAGE **155,** l. 10. *Belcher,* James (1781–1811), champion
prize-fighter before Cribb.

PAGE **156,** l. 7. *the plan,* for raising bodies of volunteers.

l. 23. *Montesquieu*: Charles de Secondat, Baron de Montesquieu, author of *De l'Esprit des Lois* (1748).

PAGE **158,** l. 24. *Whither is Europe's,* &c., the opening lines
of Akenside's Ode *To the Country Gentlemen of England,* 1758.

PAGE **160,** l. 3. *Sir James Graham.* See note to p. 129.

l. 6. *Power of Imprisonment . . . Six-Acts.* The Habeas
Corpus Act was suspended in 1817, but revived in the next
year.

l. 7. *Ellenborough's Act,* passed in 1803, making it a capital
offence to attempt violence on a gamekeeper when arresting
poachers.

Poaching Transportation Act, passed in 1816, making any
one found in a forest or chase by night, and with a poaching
net, liable to transportation for seven years.

l. 8. *New Trespass Act,* the Malicious Trespass Act of 1820,
under which any person injuring a building, hedge, tree, or
any wood or underwood paid a fine of £5, or was sent to hard
labour in a gaol for three months.

Sunday Tolls. From 1558 to 1846 any person not attending
church on a Sunday was liable to a fine of 12d. In 1625 a law
severely restricted Sunday pastimes, and a law of 1781 forbade
the use of rooms on Sunday for any amusement paid for in
money.

PAGE **162,** l. 33. *He is a Merchant,* &c. : Hosea xii. 7.

PAGE **163,** l. 20. *tithes.* See note to p. 133.

PAGE **166,** l. 25. *board wages,* wages to the minimum amount
fixed by the magistrates on the Speenhamland system : see
note on p. 113, l. 5.

l. 26. *spring guns,* guns concealed in bracken or underwood and discharged by contact, in frequent use against
poachers, and forbidden by an Act of 1827.

PAGE **168,** l. 2. *fable of La Fontaine : Le vieillard et les
trois jeunes hommes.*

PRINTED IN GREAT BRITAIN AT THE UNIVERSITY PRESS, OXFORD
BY VIVIAN RIDLER, PRINTER TO THE UNIVERSITY